Divine Messengers

Rosemary DeTrolio

Rosemary DeTrolio

2026

www.rosemaryd.com

Printed in the United States of America
First Printing 2019
First Edition 2019
ISBN: 978-1-73398693-9

<u>Dedicated</u>

To My Parents

Hands of Light by Rosemary LLC

We are, each of us angels with only one wing;

and we can only fly by embracing one another.

--Luciano De Crescenzo

Table of Contents

Chapter 1
What Are Angels?

Have a vision not clouded by fear. -- Cherokee Proverb

God is everywhere, from the smallest leaf to the tallest tree. In the darkest moment and in the most joyous hour, they are with us. Angels are God's messengers. We are all guided and helped but may be unaware of this divine connection. Angels are spiritual beings, attendants, helpers, intermediaries and messengers. They have your best interest at heart. How do I know? I've been in communication with them since 1993.

The purpose of my book is to remind you of this unseen help all around us. In the darkest hour or in the brightest one, you're never alone. The messages the angels have shared with me have changed the course of my life. Many people shared profound experiences with me.

What do angels look like?

I'll describe my own first hand visions of them. In the moment between wake and sleep, I've had the privilege to see their beautiful energy. I realized the angelic realm can appear in many different ways. When I meet with clients during an angel communication session, both of us often feel goosebumps when the angels visit. Angel vibration is so high, the hairs on my arms tingle when they are near. The angels verify information for the client in this way.

One night the angels showed themselves as sparkles of firefly lights. I've seen disembodied glowing hands in prayer floating by me. The angels transmit a warm glow. Another night, the brilliant light was so intense, I thought a high beam flashlight was pointed at my eyes. Yet another evening, I awoke to see my husband's angel praying over him. She was a stunning seven-foot winged women with golden hair and hands folded in prayer. With her, a three-inch cherub flew across the room and a bald-headed monk hovered over our bed then winked at me. As strange as these situations may sound, it's true. I felt blessed by them.

You haven't been alone on your earth journey. Many souls are awakening to the understanding we are all part of this fabric of energy. Angels exist, even if you may not have seen them.

The word awakening is as old as time itself. Every culture on earth has had spiritual people, seers, seekers, psychics, and religious teachers who have otherworldly information. Even the word 'alchemy' was a metaphor for the enlightened soul transforming lead into gold. Awakening isn't reserved for just the saints. We can all awaken. Have you seen the numbers 11:11? This numeric pattern appears to wake you to your own spiritual path. Meditation is the best way to commune with angels and to become aware.

Self-awareness is the gateway to the soul's doorway and to Universal Knowledge. The higher self is a collection of the highest gifts your own soul has mastered through each life lesson. Your higher self is also called your soul. It directly links to your intuition and to your guardian angel.

86% of the people surveyed believe in angels. The good news is that angels believe in the other 14%. Angels are non-denominational beings. Every culture has a form of winged helpers, spiritual light beings, with various names to represent the angelic forces. In the Zoroastrian faith, guardian angels are called Fravashi. In Sanskrit, they are called Avolokiteshvara, or healers. To me, angels are trusted friends who are always there to guide us.

God is everywhere, from the smallest leaf to the tallest tree. In the darkest moment and in the most joyous hour, they are with us. Angels are God's messengers. Even though we're all guided and helped, we may be unaware of this divine connection.

Angels are spiritual beings, attendants, helpers, intermediaries and messengers. They have no will of their own. Their mission is to protect, guide, and help us while we are on earth. How do I know? I've been in communication with them since 1993.

> *Your vision will become clear only when you look into your heart. Who looks outside, dreams. Who looks inside, awakens.*
>
> *-- Carl Jung*

The higher self is linked to intuitive pathways. Intuition is much more accurate than our brain or logic. It's a gut and heart knowing. This smart navigator isn't fooled, even when even when your own ego tries to talk you out of an intuitive insight. Think of the times your gut told you something felt wrong, yet you did it anyway. Did it turn out well for you? My guess is you wished you would have listened to your gut. Our spiritual nature is often lost when we overthink every decision. In a busy world and huge to-do lists, it's easy to lose sight of it.

We have free will to follow or turn away from the navigator, and many do. In receptive state, as in prayer or meditation, our soul vibrates at a much higher frequency, as in light wave oscillations. We can connect to the superlative guidance given by angels and spiritual guides with intent.

My own first angel message changed the course of my life. I was finishing the last class for my Master's degree in Education. During the night before my last elective class, I was in bed and I heard a glass window breaking. My husband and got up to search for the broken window or pane of glass, but there was none. My husband didn't hear the noise, but got up to appease me.

The next day, I attended my *Stress Management for Children* elective. During our class session, we were instructed to remain silent for the entire session just as Buddhists do when they take a vow of silence.

This frustrating exercise challenged and frustrated me. My mind chattered like static on the TV screen of my mind. After four hours of silence, my monkey-chatter mind ceased.

A sudden burst of enlightenment, a flash of divine insight flooded me. When I entered the room, I was stunned to see colors pop out around student's heads and bodies. After investigation, I learned I'd seen the aura, a colorful energy field surrounding the body. Most can't see these colors with the naked eye. This intrigued me to learn more. I reasoned, if I could see auras, maybe I could directly ask God about my path. Why not?

I took a leap of faith, prayed, and asked God, "What am I supposed to do next?" Then I recited the Our Father prayer, sat at my computer and typed a question. "God, if you need to tell me anything, send me your angelic messengers for guidance. Tell me my path and purpose. What do you want me to know?" I prayed and listened, but really didn't expect what happened to me next.

A strong bolt of energy moved through me. I sat ram-rod straight, as if a military officer just arrived and yelled, "Attention!" I didn't turn around, but felt this strong presence enter the room and stand behind me. Oddly, I had no fear of it, only respect.

My crown tingled, my skull vibrated, and the searing heat shot down my spine. Next, I received a slow, steady stream of words. Although I was fully conscious, I felt as if I were a secretary to a patient boss dictating to me at a snail's pace.

Unlike my own writing, I had no forethought about the next word I'd type or the correct way to turn a phrase. The instructions were laborious, word by word, and not completed thoughts as when I construct a story. This new process was foreign. This angel trained me to receive their communication and not miss any important words.

When I finished, I took a breath, astounded as I reread the passage. I thought, "I'm not smart enough to know this or to write this." The language and phrasing, archaic, and the style, not my own. The first communication was about assisting and guiding lost seekers find God. The message imparted information about a spiritual battle of light and darkness.

I put the message aside unsure of whom to share it with. I decided upon a non-judgmental friend of mine named Melissa. After reading the message she said, "This is a real message and it's amazing."

My trepidation about my communication didn't end there, but her words helped me feel more confident. Back in 1993, I had faith, but I also had self-doubts. After my unusual first experience, I didn't understand why I had this ability. I didn't know what to do with it. I always believed that angels existed but doubted I was worthy enough to speak with them.

I sought guidance from a minister who happened to be at the meditation day I attended with her. He verified that Angel Uriel had communicated with me. He explained Angel Uriel is the angel of salvation and fire who puts seekers on their path quickly. Uriel's energy is strong and no nonsense. Think of Uriel as a spiritual drill sergeant. At the time, I never heard this angel's name, but I felt his strong commanding presence when I received the words. Uriel is one serious angel.

The minister's explanation helped me to understand Uriel's fire and explained the searing heat on the top of my crown. He told me to pray to God, but allow Uriel's guidance to teach me. He comforted me and assured me that I had a rare opportunity to learn and I shouldn't abandon it or be afraid.

The minister explained biblical symbolism of light and darkness a reference to the Star of David. (More explanation the next section).

After the meditation seminar, I researched Angel Uriel. I learned Arch Angel Michael captured Satan, but Angel Uriel chained Satan. I received this message on Uriel's feast day... another synchronicity. I believe the synchronistic timing of this 'chance meeting' was divinely orchestrated.

Connect with God daily in your own way. Many find a safe, loving haven in their parish, temple, or place of worship. For some, the forest is the cathedral that connects to God. There's no wrong way to pray. Say a prayer anywhere. We are forever connected to God, nature, angels, and to each other.

If you begin to live life looking for the God that is all around you, every moment becomes a prayer.
-- Frank Bianco

Uriel's First Message to Me

As you read Uriel's words, notice that the first sentence is actually a metaphor for the veil between earth and the angelic realm: the 'glass wall'. I believe that this was the crash of glass I heard in my home.

Notice the style and verbiage in this reading. You'll notice it's very different from the way I write. There is no correction or rewording of any angel message either. You see it as I received it.

July 28, 1993 - My First Angel Communication

A window of glass shattered. God's door was opening to the silent mass of people waiting to hear his word. Enter the quiet and let the ideas flow in. The time has come for those who seek to hear the voice of God. He will speak to all who listen. Enter in the dragon of faith. Pierce the soul in truth and watchful eye, a shield of faith to protect you.

I am the keeper of the flame, the watcher for those who seek guidance. God's fire I keep. A pure and burning light to show the way, tarry not in your life. The time has come to reach up. Fear not for the word of God is there. Seek harmony and light through thought and deed. Venture the wheel of Solomon. Hurt not the earth or thine creatures, as he has made all of these.

Let he who hears my word enter in. Make witness to God's fury. Be of the believers to cast darkness out. Rise not the breath of the wind, the shadow of fear, the hallowed darkness of the human mind, as God's tears fall. Listen with wise ears to me. Respond, child, to the call. Cast out fear. Make haste, as the thunderous cry of the army of God will rise up against darkness.

Be of those who gather and pray, be at one and light the way. Show the fearful a light, for as those who know the answer will commence to appear. We hear your voice. God answers prayers of those who seek the truth. Don't doubt as Thomas did, the word. He was a true believer and faithful servant, but because he saw. Accept faith as your lotus, your truth, your joy. **(end)**

The "Wheel of Solomon" is an ancient symbol for the joining of the upper and lower worlds, and is a metaphysical symbol for the Star of David. The dragon is a protective symbol representing the spirit in Asian cultures.

I was excited and a little scared when I read back the incredible words I'd channeled. I wanted to share these communications with everyone, but my fear of judgement made me hesitant to do so. Would anyone believe me? Twenty-six years later, I continue to channel the angel's words. The angels have worked miracles for each person hearing their wisdom and I am forever grateful to them.

Three Years Later

Before ever channeling a word for anyone else, three years had passed. Within that time, I had learned to ask better questions to receive clear answers during my own time communicating with them.

My faith continued to be tested through life lessons. Each step taught me more about my spirit, inner strength, and faith. Angels mission is to help us all find hope, forgive others, and spread love. Each of us has a mission. We are here to complete the mission we came here to do. I would have loved an angel to burst forth in front of me. They needed my faith, not my request for proof. So it took time before I was gifted to see them.

When Uriel requested that I speak about angels in public, my free will had to agree. The angel said, "It's in your blueprint and life mission, but you could say no." The following message is an answer to my question, "Why can't everyone communicate with angels."

2001 Channeled Angel Message

If words were a beam of light, then all would receive them. The connection of human and the *angelic realm* is one of light beam and God essence. It is a natural connection and it is always present.

Why do some not connect or feel the angels?

It's a progression of readiness, a state of openness and grace. Be not the open child of God, (be closed to it) and the information, although there, will not be perceived. The openness and willingness to drop control, to allow God is the way that we allow our soul to communicate, and the angelic realm to communicate through our souls. **(end)**

If you're lucky, you'll have the honor to experience them.

Angels need not prove anything to us. They don't want to frighten us. Their appearance is a blessing. But they didn't show up due to my bidding. They exist just beyond that veil of your vision. I have no power to make them appear, no matter how much I may want validation because proof is on God's terms. The angels told me:

> *Belief comes before proof. This is faith.*

But when Jesus saw it, he was indignant and said to them, "Let the children come to me; do not hinder them, for to such belongs the kingdom of God. Truly, I say to you, whoever does not receive the kingdom of God like a child shall not enter it." And he took them in his arms and blessed them, laying his hands on them. (Mark 10:14-16)

Other people see them too

As a business owner, many people come to me for readings, Reiki session, and intuitive work. It's no surprise, I've heard many experiences from my clients. I met a woman whose three-year-old toddler had cancer. That child had a spontaneous cure after seeing an angel. Her mother shared the following story with me. One day her child looked up in her bedroom, pointed, and said, "Mommy, a beautiful lady is sending me colors to heal my sick. She said I'll get all better."

I've heard many first-hand stories from parents of children who saw angels. They are present and able to help you with your permission. When you pray and ask, you give angels permission to intercede.

After receiving hundreds of verifications of my readings, hearing repeatedly, how reading was 'life altering', I continue to be their willing secretary and servant. I could've turned away from my path, but I learned to trust the angels more than my fears.

Chapter 2
Dream Slayers, Naysayers and Skeptics

Quantum mechanics is very impressive. But an inner voice tells me that it is not yet the real thing. The theory yields a lot, but it hardly brings us any closer to the secret of the Old One. In any case I am convinced that He doesn't play dice.
-- Albert Einstein

E ven the brilliant scientific mind of Einstein believed in God. For every observation, there's a skeptic. Mine was my mother. When I told her about my experiences, she cut me short, changed the subject with a simple comment. "That's nice honey." I knew she wasn't willing to hear more. She was wary of my angel contact and I understood her reservations.

After losing an older sister to cancer years when I was very young, my mom's faith was shaken to the core. With all her prayers and faith, we still lost her. My mom never got over the pain of her loss and we all felt it. Dad was just as heartbroken, but managed to bring light into our family with his joy.

When I mentioned angels, dad deferred to mom's opinion. Dad couldn't keep up with her quick wit or sharp tongue. And she was very smart. He stated, "I hope you're not getting *loopy* with all this stuff." Even though dad's instincts were razor-sharp, mom's fear and distrust were strong, and he always deferred to her.

As coincidence would have it, my mom had a bout with ill health that wouldn't quit. Her lungs were hurting and she was convinced that she was dying. Mom was impatient with her health. She asked me, "You know those angels you *say* you can talk to? Can you ask them if I'm ok? Ask if I have lung cancer."

I agreed. The angels reported mom had scarring on her lungs from bronchitis, needed to drink more water, take fewer medications, and she needed to clear the toxins from her body. The angels told me that she needed a new lung doctor, and the next one would give her the right advice she needed about her health. Oddly enough, years later, my dad had lung cancer and eventually succumbed to it.

After sharing the angel's message with her, she nodded her head but didn't say a word. She had been to four doctors and now had one more specialist to visit. As predicted by the angels, the last doctor told her that she had scarring in the lungs, needed less medications, she needed to drink more water.

After that, mom believed me. She called to ask, "You talk to angels?" As if she didn't understand me before. My father, armed with mom's assurance, felt secure enough to give my business card out and tell everyone about my special talent.

In 2003, both of my parents attended my angel communication class. My sister, Sandy, also onboard, attended an angel class too. Like them, she tells people about me.

Since I didn't share my strange experiences with my family until later in life, I was the hidden family spiritualist. It's no wonder my childhood costume of choice was a gypsy. If everyone held the same beliefs, life would be boring. Skeptics are a confident breed and keep a watchful eye on the world.

In the Bible story of Apostle Paul, he was the world's worst skeptic ever. He sent Christians to death for their beliefs. It wasn't until God zapped Saul blind-struck that he found his own faith in God. They say when you're knocked to your knees, pray. Saul changed his name to Paul, Jesus' most passionate follower and disciple.

Think of people you know who are diagnosed with a bad illness or health issue. Sometimes a tragedy can change the course of a life in profound ways.

Skeptics want to believe but they also require proof. But faith isn't about proof, it's about belief in what we can't prove.

For some, skepticism is false comfort, a control mechanism over a messy unexplained world. Life is messy and not all experiences fit into the tidy box tied with a big red bow.

There's a choice. Some will throw away the unexplained experience. Some will wait for the other shoe to drop and expect the worst. Other's will seek and explanation. It's up to us.

Skeptics evoke fear and caution. They don't mean to scare people but they are notorious for shooing away other people's experiences and beliefs. They instruct us not to be foolhardy or gullible. They remind us to fact-find. We need skeptics, but they too need us more. We encourage them to find the enlightened path in their own way.

Then there's Apostle Thomas, also known as 'Doubting Thomas.' He asked to see the wounds on Jesus's hands after Jesus appeared before him after his death. That's a skeptic if there ever was one! Jesus showed his palms but Thomas reminds us it's OK to doubt, but it's better to believe. Angel Uriel told me not to be like Thomas and doubt the word.

> *28 And Thomas answered and said unto him, My Lord and my God.*
> *29 Jesus saith unto him, Thomas, because thou hast seen me, thou hast believed: blessed [are] they that have not seen, and [yet] have believed.*

We all have skeptics and naysayers in our lives. They'll have advice you didn't ask for. They'll question your experiences or eye roll. There's a bit of Thomas in all of us.

Like Thomas, I didn't want to appear foolish or crazy, but my experience happened. Maybe you've had an unusual experience too. But believe me, through the years I've heard stories from many sane and credible people. Spiritual experiences are more widespread than you'd imagine. I chose to share my experiences with those who are open and positive.

Despite my initial personal trepidation, I forged ahead with my path. I trusted my inner guidance and the angels. At the early stages of my journey, I would have welcomed an angel to appear in front of me. I had no hard proof until I walked each step and channeled their guidance.

Angels appear if they have a message and a reason to do so.

Through the years, I've met my share of skeptics. Once I work with them, they believe, too.

Fear abounds. When someone heard I'd been talking to angels, a woman who overheard felt compelled to caution me. So, I went to my angels and asked their advice on the matter.

1999 Angel Message

A friend told me channeling is not safe. Please give me your advice on this matter. How do I respond and stay safe?

It is wise to protect yourself with light at all times. The power of goodness is strong, but open circuits (this means a soul who is very sensitive) can ground negative entities, just as lightning grounds to earth.

Be wise and pray. Be open to loving light entities. Your wisdom is keen, though humans don't always do what is wise. God granted us intuition to filter though the dark and light. You will know the feel of a dark energy and you will know the truth. **(end)**

When the solution is simple, God is answering.
                                        -Albert Einstein

God is a comedian playing to an audience too afraid to laugh.
                          -Voltaire Francois-Marie Arouet

Life Lessons and Earth School

"Am I done with these life lessons yet?" Clients have asked me this question many times. The quick answer is no. That's why we're on earth.

Only God knows when we finish learning. My suspicion is we are always learning and growing. We learn throughout eons of time even in spirit form. The angels assured me this belief is true. The purpose of life lessons is to evolve and transform our never-ending spiritual growth spurt. We co-create with God.

Lessons appear wearing different faces, places, situations, and events. Lessons change or diminish once we surrender and understand what to do. We call these lessons problems or mistakes, but the angels call them opportunities.

We often create patterns and loops which stop spiritual growth. Think of a life lesson or situation that continues to repeat. When we stubbornly refuse to learn from our experiences, the lesson stays until we get it.

Think of those people you know who continually chose the same path which leads to distress and unhappiness. Choosing the same wrong action is a block, an addictive pattern, or unlearned life lesson. If you notice a repeating pattern of events in your life, it's a red flag waving at you to change your direction and harness a new opportunity.

We all see God, the conscious life force in different our own way. It doesn't matter what you call God or your higher power. This loving energy is available to all of us.

I see God as a force of light, an energy being that infuses everything and everyone. We are all connected by this conscious force of light. I understand Jesus to be a human man while on earth, who housed a perfected soul of light. He was a wise teacher, a soul, an avatar, a higher being sent to teach us a better way.

Once Jesus died, his body transitioned to become part of the expansive light force we call God, *as we all do when our souls pass over.* The message Jesus showed us is simple. We are all eternal beings; we cross over into light, our consciousness survives, and we have to accept the truth of this immortality.

Where does it leave us? Every human has a conscious soul which transcends death. People in the medical field study near death experiences. There's new information coming out of Columbia University since many heart patients have been revived. Even brain-dead people who have been revived experience visits by loved ones, angels, and guides. Each one said they felt peaceful and loved. All who returned were told it wasn't their time to cross over.

Through my classes, I have met many people comfortable enough to share their near-death Experiences (NDE). Two women I met informed me that they saw angels, deceased family members, and experienced intense bright light upon passing over. Both women had a choice whether to stay or come back to earth. Angels instructed them to return to earth. Each had a choice to stay or go. Their free will was still present even in death.

A friend of mine saw the face of her future husband and future children while she received last rites. I met a former trucker pronounced dead at an accident and then returned to describe his conversation with an angel. It changed the course of his life. After his NDE, he quit his job spent his time creating angelic music and art to help guide people back to God.

While at an event, I saw a man with a brilliant blue aura. I knew he must have a story, so I asked him why I saw such a brilliant clear light around him. He told me he had crossed over during a heart operation. After meeting Jesus and his angels, he changed his life, stopped working in the corporate world, and now makes healing wands with crystals to help people clear their energy field.

In each case, the NDE person realigned their life and had a clear sense of purpose and strong belief in the afterlife. Each person longed to return to the pure love they felt on the other side.

We can easily forgive a child who is afraid of the dark. The real tragedy of life is when men are afraid of the light.

– Plato

Rosemary DeTrolio

Chapter 3
Divine Timing is God's Pocket Watch

Divine timing means in the right time. Patience isn't easy for a person who dives into projects, like I do. But God's timing and my timing are not the same. God answers prayers because he/she sees the big picture and we don't. Like a ripple effect, one answered prayer can affect other people in its wake.

I've met countless people who lost jobs they despised. At first, it seemed tragic. But the job loss caused each person to make a changes.

My sister's decision to remain in a sales job she disliked brought about a health issue. She was forced to take a leave and have an operation. While recuperating, she realized her time away was just what she needed to gain a new perspective. She decided to leave her job, even forgoing the security. She started her own successful design business and now her life is happy and lucrative, and healthy.

Think of relationships. When first marriage was heading for divorce, I prayed for my marriage to improve, but it ended anyway. At the time I couldn't see a bright future. Now I'm happily married and my life turned out better than I could have imagined.

Pray for your highest good *but not for a particular outcome*. When we allow God to move in our lives, it's called *surrender*. Life is our perspective. You can view an issue as a problem or an opportunity to grow.

After a trip to the islands where I saw people jammed into a one room tin shacks, my tiny home seemed like a castle. The following African fable is a good story about perspective.

The Mice and The Big Animal

There was a colony of mice worried about the large animal that stood in front of their home.

"What is it?" The leader mouse wondered. "I think we should form a committee and decide!"

Each mouse ran to a different part of the strange creature. The first mouse climbed on top of it. Another mouse stayed near the front. Another stood behind it. After each mouse decided the right answer, they regrouped at the bottom of the animal.

"I saw a tail animal. It's the world's most giant tail."

"No, you're wrong. It is an ear-animal. I saw a huge flapping ear."

"You're both wrong. It is a foot-to-nail animal," said another.

One mouse stood on its back to declare, "This is a mountain, not an animal."

They began to argue. The more they argued, the more they stubbornly insisted that they were right.

Before long, the mice were biting at each other and soon they were at war. Each mouse attempted to convert the others to their right way of thinking. Some mice wanted to build a wall to keep the bad mice out.

The tiniest mouse was so tired of all the fighting, retreated to the top of a tree to think and meditate.

When he looked out, he saw the whole animal. He realized the mice were right and also wrong. He was so exciting, he ran down to share his vision.

"Excuse me," said the littlest mouse, "I saw big ears, a tail, and a mountainous body. I saw all the things you saw. Each of you had a piece of the truth, but no one saw the big picture. Climb the tree with me and look at the big creature."

Some open-minded mice climbed the tree and saw a whole new truth. It was like the light went on and they'd been in the dark. Others stayed in fear and self-righteousness and fought wars with each other.

***

There are so many religions, dogmas, and paths. Like the mice, we see a small piece of God's truth. Religions, cultures, and paths are different. Each faith is a giant spoke of the wheel. The Universal truth is in its center. Just like those mice, we all see one spoke of the wheel. Isn't it pointless to argue and fight over a limited understanding of the truth?

The following prayer has helped me to focus upon this universal truth.

God send me light and understanding. Help me to decide the best course of action and help me to choose the path of greatest joy. Let it be for the highest good and intention for all concerned. I sent this prayer out to God for _____.
I ask that it be answered for the highest good of all concerned.

Intuition

Intuition is a natural ability. All of us have it. With practice, it can become stronger. When we listen to our intuition it continues to guide us. I've learned to obey my inner guidance, the small voice within.

I've learned the hard way when I didn't listen to my intuitive warnings I'd get a cosmic slap on the hand. We can choose the easy way or the hard way to learn; I've done both.

When we learn from life's lessons, situations will drop away leaving us wiser for the experience. Be inflexible and it'll be like throwing a monkey wrench in the cosmic machinery. Forcing will doesn't work. The outcome isn't good and that's the hard way.

Be aware of repeating patterns. Did you ever notice that if you have an issue with dominant people, they'll appear everywhere? Did you ever notice that impatience leads to myriads of situations requiring every ounce of it you have? Did you ever notice when you judge others, you are also judged?

The universe acts like a mirror reflecting us. Think of a giant matrix where we exist inside, only we are unaware. The world is a holographic matrix of energy and each soul imprints this energy field. Make sure each day your mirror shines back a face you are proud to wear.

We, like all things in a holographic universe are ultimately a frequency phenomenon which our mind converts into various holographic forms.

Michael Talbot (from Holographic Universe)

I want to know how God created this world. I am not interested in this or that phenomenon, in the spectrum of this or that element. I want to know His thoughts; the rest are details.

-- Albert Einstein

Angel Connections & Creativity

We don't have to die to experience angels. Creativity is the secret passageway to the divine. Create music, draw, or write, and you will allow guidance from your angels to flow. Meditation and inner sparks ignite their communication with you. If you think you can't draw or write, try it anyway. You might surprise yourself. Art opens intuitive doorways.

Creativity doesn't need approval. Don't judge your final product, but learn to enjoy self-expression. Don't concern yourself with people's opinions of your creation. Art is self-expression.

Many adults and children are trapped in self-depreciation and self-judgement. The beauty of the final product isn't the reason to create. It's the process of creation and how you choose to express your unique self.

Life is a creative process. We co-create by intention, thoughts and perceptions. Be grateful. According to Abraham Hicks, any thought you hold for seventeen seconds will manifest. This is the basis for Law of Attraction— and it works.

Do you hold bad thoughts for seventeen seconds? Do you worry for seventeen seconds? If so, you are using the Law of Attraction in the negative.

Practice to break this habit. When a scary thought arrives say, "I cancel and delete my negative thought." Then replace it with a new positive thought. For instance, when I worry about my son's travels, I delete the worry and say, "My son is in God's hands, safe and secure. The Protective light of angels surround him everywhere he goes." Next, I visualize a protective light around him.

Our thoughts are a shopping list of our desires. Suppose you went to the food store for healthy foods, but came home with junk food. Your mind wrote healthy foods on the list, but your true intention selected junk food. Your intention writes your shopping list. Your desire, intention, and actions give the list power. Consider what you really want to bring into your life. Focus emotion, intent, and actions upon it.

Be careful and aware of energies you send out. Energy has the natural ability to bind to itself. Negative thinking patterns work the same way. If you hear someone say, "Nothing good ever happens," they'll be right, and it will add to your shopping list.

Energy isn't good or bad, it's a request and signal you send to the Universe. What we focus on increases. Where thought goes, energy flows. Both positive and negative thoughts hold remarkable energy within them. Like attracts like. Listen to your thoughts and your requests. Soon, you'll notice your own pattern of thinking. What are you writing on your shopping list?

Manifestation is powerful. This means we co-create with God. Think about that. When I first learned of this truth, I reviewed all the life lessons I had requested without knowing. Why did I find myself in frustrating situations? Unwittingly, I'd written wanting more patience on my shopping list. I got what I'd asked for, many opportunities to practice patience through the frustrating situations I'd requested.

The Power of Music

Energy and vibration connect music, sound, color, and light. Each has vibration and frequency, just like we do. Did you notice when you are relaxed flashes of insight pop into your mind? It happens to me when I'm driving or taking a shower.

Sometimes a song plays on the radio sparking a memory or idea. I might see a license plate with a word on it which mirrors my thoughts. 've seen LOVE, HOPE, ANGELS, and SAM, my dad's name.

Many people told me a certain song about speaking to angels played on the radio right after leaving my angel class.

I like to connect with my angels in the morning. If I am channeling a message for someone else, I pray first, then get a downloaded message. The angels will often pop in to say hello when I'm driving. Once I was on the highway traveling at 60 mph. My angels decided it would be a dandy time to answer a question I asked them earlier in the morning. Words flowed into my head like a raging river.

"Wait! I'm driving!" I said, as I frantically pulled over to jot their messages on a cardboard tissue box. After that day, I prayed, "God you're my co-pilot, but I'm still holding that wheel. Please wait until I'm home before the angels download a message."

Have you noticed that when you are in the shower, washing dishes, or driving, you've had a great idea? When our mind is calm and receptive and are most open to guidance.

In the past, I've had difficulty clearing monkey chatter from my brain long enough to meditate. That's why channeling is easier for me. The monkeys in my brain are happy when they have a purpose to fulfill.

If you can't stay still, try walking and breathing. It's a calming meditative practice. Yoga is wonderful, too. Try mindfully washing dishes or pulling weeds. These mindless chores allow the chatter to reset. Create your own meditative moments. Wordless music shifts the mind out of left brain thinking and into right brain creativity mode.

Drawing, painting, and needlework are also a kind of meditative state. Some people love to knit. Any repetitive and easy activity will allow a gentle shift of focus. See which one works best for you.

Thoughts are Things

Since we are all part of the giant ocean of energy, we are all connected. We hold the ocean in a droplet of our soul. Our thoughts and emotions imprint the field of energy. I heard of a recent study on TV about heart energy. We can measure the collective energy of the emotion which can be measured in outer space using special instrumentation. Our feelings effect the aura around the earth! Collective consciousness makes sense, doesn't it?

https://www.heartmath.org/research/science-of-the-heart/energetic-communication/

Maurice Sendak had it right. In his book, *Where the Wild Things Are,* a youngster dreams of scary beasts personifying his angry thoughts.

Our fears are those scary things we create. Until we make friends with them, they wreak havoc with our emotions. Mind monsters are memories or thoughts living in the past. But they only exist in the mind. Without fear, we are open to a state of joyous childlike state of heightened awareness. And it's fun!

Be ready for surprises. Many times, I have reached in a pocket down to my last dollar to find a crumpled $20 bill. How wonderful to receive a check, unexpected present or act of goodwill. God moves through us. Pray for the highest good and allow God to answer prayers that meet the highest good for all.

Who, What, Where, and Why the Wild Things Are
by Beverly Botelho

You got one thing right, Mr. Sendak—

The Wild Things are usually smiley.

But the beasts I've known have done terrible,

Horrible, unforgiveable things.

Think Hitler, think Pol Pot, think Idi Amin.

You got another thing right, Mr. Sendak—

The beasts are the ones who control by decree.

The beasts and the dictators become indistinguishable.

You never asked any of the questions the journalist would

have asked, Mr. Sendak.

And around the globe:

The beasts are not the ones across the sea, on the nightly

news, around the block.

They're not the institutions that teach us, the bodies that

govern us, the media that feed us.

The real Wild Things are the appetites that drive us,

the senses that lie to you.

The hearts that beat inside us all.

Attitude of Gratitude

Make a gratitude journal. Noticing and writing all your blessings will uplift your energy and shift you into a state of grace. Thoughts create energy. Be mindful of how you carry yourself, what you think, and what you say. Our thoughts carry energy which can influence the field of energy around us. We are all connected.

Thoughts create forms of energy that pattern in the ethers and then land and collect in the astral realm. I found an interesting article I've included below along with a link to the original article. Our thoughts add to the Universal Field called Collective Consciousness. Don't allow your own wild things to take over your serenity.

What is the Astral Realm?

You know all those negative thoughts we have? They are dense and heavy thoughts that hang out in the astral realm. Nightmares, scary images, all thought forms from the energy of our minds imprint the ethers. This realm can't hurt us, but it's sticky and has a low vibration. Like smog over a city, the realm is gray and colorless. Fear and worry make mind monsters. They add to your distress if you let it.

Low thoughts imprint this ocean of energy, snagged into the astral plane like a sticky net. Think of the nightly news. All you hear broadcast is fear and trepidation. The news creates fear until you believe you are never safe in the world.

Negative worries are psychic sludge. Heavy, unpleasant, and depressed energy is not buoyant, so it drops like sewage into the concentric ring hovering a few feet above earth. I've seen it in my dreams. The realm is superimposed a few feet above the earth, but it's gray and dismal.

Lost souls, known as ghosts, inhabit the astral realm. They too are temporarily stuck, depressed, and hopeless. In movies, you may have seen ghosts 'floating' off the ground. Their soul is not buoyant enough to lift away from it. Negative thoughts weigh souls down like a person dragging a rock behind him. Once a soul has made a choice to awaken, the angels help the soul raise above the astral plane, lifting them up and out. Enlightened Energy imprints the Collective Consciousness. Choose to imprint joy.

100th Monkey Study by Ken Keyes

The Japanese monkey, *Macaca fuscata,* has been observed in the wild for a period of over 30 years. In 1952, on the island of Koshima, scientists were providing monkeys with sweet potatoes dropped in the sand. The monkeys liked the taste of the raw sweet potatoes, but they found the dirt unpleasant.

An 18-month-old female named Imo found she could solve the problem by washing the potatoes in a nearby stream. She taught this trick to her mother. Her playmates also learned this new way and they taught their mothers, too. This cultural innovation was gradually picked up by various monkeys before the eyes of the scientists.

Between 1953 and 1958 all of the young monkeys learned to wash the sandy sweet potatoes to make them more palatable. Only the adults who imitated their children learned this social improvement. Other adults kept eating the dirty sweet potatoes. Then something startling took place. In the autumn of 1958, a certain number of Koshima monkeys were washing sweet potatoes – the exact number is not known.

Let us suppose that when the sun rose one morning there were 99 monkeys on Koshima Island who had learned to wash their sweet potatoes. Let us further suppose that later that morning the hundredth monkey learned to wash potatoes. By that evening almost everyone in the tribe was washing sweet potatoes before eating them.

The added energy of the hundredth monkey somehow created an ideological breakthrough! A most surprising thing observed by these scientists was that the habit of washing sweet potatoes then jumped over the sea. Colonies of monkeys on other islands and the mainland troop of monkeys at Takasakiyama began washing their sweet potatoes.

Chapter 4
Guide or Angel?

Guide and angel energy are different and feel different. Angel energy is light and uplifting, while guide energy is earthy, and much like talking to another person.

Names and human personalities are no longer attached to the high guide. Angels have no ego at all, only God's will. The spirit of the human guide works to eliminate ego and be of service. In many cases, the guide's soul has earned the right to be of service to the living human and has had many incarnations of practice. He or she continues to learn by helping others on earth. This is an honor a soul earns.

A high guide[1] strives to eliminate ego, increase their own soul's light by helping others, and to progress forward and not give much information about who they were in one or two lifetimes. They see the big picture and no longer hold attraction for earthly goods. Loved ones may guide, visit, and love you, but they are not necessarily high guides unless they have earned the right through many past incarnations.

Your loved ones that visit are not ghosts, but spirits. They can come and go as they please. Some work out karma and forgiveness with you,

---

[1] High guide is a reference to a learned soul with a higher soul vibration imprint.

some are there to check on you and lend support. Many times, they will show up in dreams to comfort or to visit with you.

What is a Spirit Guide?

A high spiritual guide guides refers to a deceased soul of a higher soul vibration than your own. A guide chooses to assist the living person to help them grow spiritually. Just like a teacher with many students, a spiritual guide may have several humans in his or her charge. And just like students, we have different capacities to understand or to learn. A deceased relative, such as a beloved grandparent may guide you, but is not usually considered a high spiritual guide. Most likely, it's not a soul you knew in this lifetime.

Why does a guide choose to help us? By helping humans on earth, the guide's soul progresses too. Since guides were once human, they understand our concerns in a very different way than an angel would understand them. Many mediums work with guides who help link them to souls on the other side.

High guides are more spiritually aware than the person they assist, therefore, they have a different view of how to solve a certain situation and can lead to the right resource, person, or place.

As you advance spiritually, your soul is able to attract a guide with a higher vibration, one that is closer to your own. Like attracts like. The guide needs to be in resonance with the person they guide and teach at a level which is right for you.

Just as you advance grades at school, different guides will step forward as needed and change as you advance. If you chose to learn the Reiki system of healing (the one I use and teach), Reiki guides are assigned to each student as they progress.

I had channeled angels for three years before I'd agree to speak to my guides. I was comfortable with angel energy, but wary of guide energy. Before I agreed to work with guides, I sought permission from my angels and asked that they oversee all interactions with guides. Angels helped me discern if a guide was a good fit for me.

Guides were once human; therefore, have a human influence and sound to their advice. High guides will remind you about free will and won't interfere in your decision making.

Low guides will directly tell you what to do and interfere with your free will. This information is no better than trusting a stranger down the street for advice. Sometimes a ghost will masquerade as a guide fooling an unexperienced person. Angels and high guides will never ask you to harm anyone or give up your free will.

High vibration guides will lower their vibration to match with yours. It's like tuning in to a radio station at just the right frequency. The higher the soul vibration is within the human, the more easily to magnetically attract or match a higher vibration guide.

High guides work closely with the angel realm. They are not perfect beings, but strive to assist. The longer a soul has been a spiritual guide, the less interested they are with their own earthly past.

The Bible cautions people against 'speaking to spirits' because if you aren't clear enough or have the right intention, are mentally unbalanced, addicted, or untrained, you might attract lost souls or entities instead of a guide. This is harmful to you as a lost soul might take advantage of your fears and worries unbeknownst to you. Your own fears carry a vibration and imprint your energy field. Like attracts like.

How do you know your vibration is low?

Depression, sadness, desperation all have a very low vibrational rate. Love, joy, optimism have a quick and positive vibration rate. That's why exhaustion takes over when a person is having sad or stressful emotions.

Therefore, a person with a low vibration can unintentionally attract a low guide, astral spirit, or ghost and should not attempt to contact guides, ghosts, or lost spirits. I met a client who came to me very distraught. She believed she was channeling "a high guide" who turned out to be a nasty entity who played upon her fears and insecurities. This was a big red flag. Angels and guides will never impart negative feelings or information to the human. They don't play into fears or stroke your ego.

She asked me if she should follow the harmful advice this entity imparted. Of course, I said, "No."

Angels can visit and comfort any person regardless of their vibration since they will raise us up and comfort us in times of need. Their presence alone can bolster your soul's vibration, much like a caring friend would.

Angel energy affects us much in the way a tuning fork finds its own vibration. The higher pitch and vibration can tune up the lower tone. Think of two tuning forks matching tones. This is known as resonance, or frequency resonance. Chose hopeful and optimist people to lift your own vibration and mood.

A higher vibration guide resonates with joy and hope. Information they impart will always be for your highest good *as well as the good of others*. At no time will a spiritual guide or angel tell you to do something directly as these breaks the law of free will.

I advise my clients to work with angel energy first until they can discern the difference between energies. Protect yourself by setting intention, praying, and grounding your body by the feet.

I insist on using prayer and protection practices even during meditation. During meditation, the crown chakra is wide open and a person is most open to outside influences if they are not trained to sit in their own power and connect with the Higher Self or angelic forces.

Angel energy is loving, safe, and uplifting. I've spoken to people who let unsavory spirits or guides into their space and couldn't discern the difference. Not all otherworldly influences are positive ones. Just because a soul is dead, it doesn't mean it's any smarter than you are. The next part is from a recent angel reading I did for a good friend of mine.

Angel Communication from 2019

The Matrix resonates with the frequency of love, the sound and vibration of love. Since love is stronger than any other vibrations, it can override discordant energies in the field. The higher vibrations can 'blast' lower ones away, much like glass shatters with a high-pitched clear tone. Low vibration energy can be shattered, such as cancerous cells and the incoming method of radio ablation. We see an influx of new ideas and a connection to soul information regarding areas of thought and vibrational medicine. Vibration links to body mechanics, healing, and vibrational patterns for health, and *earth matrix*. There is also a holographic matrix around the earth which holds a pattern which also houses a frequency banding the earth. The frequency of "health" or disease is imprinted on this matrix as it mirrors the energy of consciousness of humans and the energy consciousness of the earth's health. Consider two overlapping screens of awareness and like a sandwich, both are interwoven in the fabric of the matrix. (end)

An angel is a being of light and consciousness formed by God to serve as guides, mentors, protectors, and messengers. They have no free will, only the will of God. We have free will, and that's the major difference between angels and humans.

They communicate mind to mind. Each soul who is brave enough to walk this earth comes in with a specific angel, which is our guardian angel. This angel's mission is to hold your blueprint plan and support you so that you can complete your plan.

They also protect us from harm the best they are able. If we jump out of a plane without a parachute and die, it's on us. Angels do protect us, but we can override them.

Think of the brushes with death, the accidents you almost had, but didn't. I can recall at least five of my own.

Sometimes an illness or tragedy befalls someone we love. Each soul has a particular exit point, but there are early exits along the path. We don't know the final one, at least not until we are close to it. My father knew the day before he'd be leaving earth. My mom told me she had a few months to live when her time neared.

Saint Therese, The Little Flower of Jesus

Saints can guide us. We can petition them to help us.

My mother's friend told me she prays to Saint Therese and gave me a prayer card years ago. At twenty-three, I was a bit skeptical of any saint who'd send me roses for an answered prayer.

Therese Martin was the last of nine children born in 1873 in France. She entered the Carmelite convent at 15, devoting her life to God. Her "little way" was to send roses to devoted seekers who pray to her. She helps you by praying on your behalf. If she hears your prayer, she'll send you a rose. Most often it's a yellow rose, but it can come in many colors and forms.

Mom's friend directed me to pray to St. Therese before 11:00 am. She instructed me to wait three days, and see what happens. She showed me a bowl of roses, her collection of answered prayers. That was great for her, but would it happen for me? She insisted that all prayers are heard and answered in three to four days. If the prayer is granted, Saint Therese will send a yellow rose to you. Sometimes a different color rose might arrive, or a rose in another form. I had faith, but a bit of Apostle Thomas in me.

True to my brash nature at my young age, I prayed, but asked for a blue rose. Snarky, right? Why would I do such a thing? Why not pray and have faith?

Three days later, my former mother-in-law gave me a gift. It was a hair clip with a blue rose on it! She had no idea I was saying the prayer. That was the day Saint Theresa hooked me and I stopped being skeptical.

A few years later, I prayed for a healthy child. Two days later, a co-worker presented me with a red rose bush, a blessing because I was leaving the district to move to another town. Soon, I was employed in a new district.

During the third month of my pregnancy, I contracted pink eye, a fever and a severe cough, so bad, I feared I'd lose the infant I was carrying. I prayed to God, then called upon Saint Therese before falling into an exhausted sleep.

In the first trimester of my pregnancy, she was carrying a bouquet of flowers. She appeared in a dream to tell me I carried boy. Then she asked me if I wanted the baby *even if I'd be raising him alone.* This was a strange question. Why would she ask it? I answered without hesitation. "Yes, of course! I love my child."

Then I heard a booming voice say, "It is done."

When I awakened, I wondered about the message about raising the child alone. I'd been married for less than six years and thought I'd stay married for the long haul. My intuition told me something was wrong. My former husband spent many nights away working late in the city .In June, in my ninth month, I went in my yard to see my red rose bush bloomed a white flower. On the fourth day, I went out to my yard. The red rose bush in my yard bloomed one perfect white flower, the only time this ever occurred. My first-grade students drew roses for me and the coincidences piled up.

Less than a year later, on Christmas Day, my husband told me he was leaving me. My son was six months old to the day. I called upon Saint Therese with a desperate prayer for courage, to be a good mom, and for a sign that I'd be fine on my own. I remembered the white rose. I knew without a doubt; my prayers were answered.

Since that day, I have roses that filled buckets. Please don't pray for blue roses on my account. Pay close attention to the signs you get and don't be a smart aleck like me.

On my first year raising my son, my parents visited Italy. I prayed to Saint Therese for their safe travel and return. On the day I prayed, my parents entered a beautiful church in Italy. Mom called me that evening to share the following story. She told me she saw a man tending roses outside the church said to him in Italian, "My daughter would love a rose from this church." He handed her a rose and said, "Tell your daughter God blesses her and Saint Therese sends her this rose."

When my parents entered the church, they were astonished. They entered the Church of Saint Therese, the little flower of God. Mom knew I'd been praying for her intercession. She said a statue of the saint stood in the foyer of the church. The saint held a bouquet of roses in her arms, just as I dreamed of her. I treasure the rose from Italy.

Once I was back at work, Saint Therese was still working her grace. The art teacher in my school in my new school district gave me a beautiful angel holding a rose.

"Wow, you've answered my prayer. Do you know about Saint Therese?" I asked. Her eyes welled up and she handed me a card with Saint Therese's prayer on it. She told me she prays to her and had ten cards to share. A priest told her that God would let her know who would receive each card.

A friend of mine, named Theresa also says her prayer. One day, she visited the shrine of Saint Therese and brought me a rose petal from her shrine feeling guided.

My mom's neighbor passed along a rose petal to my mom told mom she was guided to give it to me. It was from the shrine dedicated to Saint Therese. Neither person knew I prayed to her, but each time, I got a rose.

Then, there was a chain letter sent to my house. When I opened it, there was the prayer to St. Therese inside sent by a stranger. I received this random letter four times from four different locations from strangers.

I have a huge glass container loaded with roses from prayers I said. My office has a blue and white theme and I have blue silk roses in my Reiki room to remind me of faith. I've recently learned that the blue rose is a sign of Jesus' Mother Mary, the woman of compassion.

If you see the blue rose, now you know why it's special to me. My name also has Rose in it, and my middle name is Theresa. My parents named me with the perfect moniker. I have many, many more stories. If you'd like to try the prayer, I have included it for you.

Without faith, life is like wearing foggy glasses on a sunny day. Faithful people believe in God, therefore will also *notice* the proof that others scoff at as coincidence.

Miraculous Invocation to Saint Therese

O Glorious Saint Therese, whom Almighty God has raised up to aid and counsel mankind, I implore your Miraculous Intercession. So powerful are you in obtaining every need of body and soul our Holy Mother Church proclaims you a "Prodigy of Miracles… the Greatest Saint of Modern Times." Recite the prayer in the morning before 11:00 am.

Novena to Saint Therese

Now I fervently beseech you to answer my petition (mention here) and to carry out your promises of "spending Heaven doing good upon earth, of letting fall from Heaven a Shower of Roses".

Henceforth, dear Little Flower, I will fulfill your plea "to be made known everywhere" and I will never cease to lead others to Jesus through you.~ Amen

Chapter 5
Ghosts and Spirit Visitors

There are many theories about ghosts. Some mediums I've met believe that all souls cross over and only the stuck part of their ego stays earthbound. Others say the soul has chosen not to enter the tunnel of light and remains stuck in the astral plane. I'm sure parts of both are true.

In my understanding, ghosts are lost souls that have turned away from the tunnel of light due to fear, an earthly connection to something here, or additive behaviors not broken while on the earth plane.

The angels told me if a soul is stuck, as soon as he or she opens to God or surrenders, the angels pull the soul into the tunnel and bring them back home (home meaning the other side).

> *Ghosts are just unhappy people with no skin...*

Everyone has free will and so does a soul. Our own free will punishes us, not God. Our soul can choose to go or stay. A ghost is a prisoner holding the key to their own cell. Some don't know they're dead, or perhaps they are attached to an earthly possession or person. Maybe the person is self-punishing, thinking they are unworthy or unforgiven. Perhaps they didn't believe in an afterlife. To feel safe, the soul stays earthbound where everything is familiar.

A ghost is a soul that has chosen not to go through the tunnel of light. Why? Some souls remain attached to earthly places or possessions through greed, and continue to inhabit their former residence not willing to give it up. We think of this as a haunting. Sometimes, a soul doesn't know or won't accept its death. Perhaps guilt holds a deceased soul near to a loved one pining for them.

A lost soul needs to believe in a force greater than their own ego. How can you help? Pray for the person or pray for all souls lost and hurting. I believe our prayers can break through this barrier.

If someone has died under tragic circumstances, remind them of your love, but encourage them to find God's love and leave you to move on. The same goes for anyone in your life to whom you were close. Free them to take the next part of their journey.

Because free will is a universal law, it applies even in death. A deceased soul must ask for help in order to move from the astral plane back into the tunnel of light making a conscious free will decision to move on.

Spirit mediums can help a stuck soul crossover but our prayers can help a soul move on too. Angels will assist the stuck soul as soon as they ask for help.

Occasionally, a lost soul latches on to my energy field attracted to its light. I sense and hear a buzzing noise on the left side of my head right before it hops into my crown.

A few times, caught off-guard, I was so exhausted I couldn't keep my eyes open. As soon I figured out what had happened, I took a salt bath and meditated demanding the soul to leave my energy field. I stated it had no permission to attach to me so it left.

If I didn't understand what was happening to me, I would've guessed I had chronic fatigue or a strange illness. My energy would have continued to drain. This story isn't to make you afraid, but to be aware that we have control over our emotions and our energy field. Please know that nothing is out to get you. We can be our own worst enemy. Ghosts are opportunists attracted to lousy moods and negativity. Once I shifted my mood and prayed, I was an unattractive host for anything negative.

In essence, the attachment taught me the power of my mood.

Prayer protects. No negative entity wants to be stuck to a faithful person. Prayer is the best way to oust them. You also have to state, "If any soul has attached to my energy field, I order you to leave now!" Ask Arch Angel Michael to help you. Say a prayer, and know you are protected.

Some ghosts think we want them to stay around us, thinking we've agreed to its presence. Our compassion response can work against us. If you feel badly for a lost soul, help cross it over; don't agree to carry it around with you like an old piece of luggage.

Ghost or spirit?

There are different views on these words. I believe all souls have opportunity to cross into the light right away. Some use free will to turn away from the light until they are ready to accept their lessons. Souls that cross over right away are spirits that can visit us, but are mostly cleared of old emotions. Souls that stay earthbound and haven't been cleared through the tunnel of light and visit 'home,' are earthbound ghosts.

Without a visit 'home', a ghost remains attached to lower vibration emotions, such as fear, anger, and greed. The ghost may stay earthbound due to an over-attachment to a person, land or objects.

Many people walk around with attachments unaware of their uninvited hitchhiker. We have the power on earth, so have no fear. Our free will and prayer protect the energy field. Ghosts are not harmful unless a person has an addiction.

If an addicted soul passes without recovery, some may choose to stay earthbound to seek the thrill they miss. If so, they will attach to a human host to feel the emotion and high. These ghosts are attracted to addictive energy feeding off his or her addictive nature. For the living host, it makes sobriety a challenge unless they seek a higher power. It's customary for AA meetings to begin with intention to heal, and to end with the Our Father prayer. This prayer raises vibration and clears entities.

Spirits of our loved ones sometimes zap bulbs too. They are just visiting and aren't earthbound or stuck. I'm convinced that my friend short-circuited his cellar lights in his own home on the day he died.

After a heartfelt prayer one night, the angel music globe in my bedroom started to play on its own. This had never happened before or since.

Read *Relax, it's only a Ghost.*[2] by Echo Bodine. Her book gives helpful advice about clearing ghost from space, but I suggest finding someone who knows how to do this in a safe way. A ghost is a soul who chose to avoid the tunnel of light and remain earthbound. Since the soul is earthbound or didn't feel loved, souls they hold resentments, anger, unfinished business, and unhealed hurt. No wonder they are miserable. The more negative they are, the heavier the soul, so it remains.

Remember, earth is our realm, not theirs. Light is always stronger than darkness. Trust God and don't fear discarnate souls.

God gives all souls salvation and forgiveness. We have free will, even in our earthly death. We must be willing to pass into the tunnel of light to free ourselves from our own lower natures.

I have been visited by lost souls. If a soul winds up in my room at night, I pray and convince the person they'll be safe, loved, and forgiven and they need to cross over. I call upon Arch angel Michael to help me. But this isn't my chosen path, so I don't seek out ghost clearings.

The soul must surrender to allow the angels to bring themselves to God. You'll have to decide which theory resonates with you. Our loved ones don't become angels, since angels were never human, but they can visit you in your dreams, or if you're open to it, they can give you a message. Think of the uncanny song on the radio, the penny, or other coincidence which reminds you of your loved one.

---

[2] http://echobodine.com/

There are also theories that our souls can visit realms of the ethers as part of our education. For instance, 'earth angels' visit the angelic realm and incarnate on earth to be of service, while others may be with forest elves, for example. It's interesting to theory to research if you are interested.

You may notice the difference of style in the communication from angel to guide. When I communicate with angels or guides, the crown chakra on top of my head opens to allow divine energy to flow in. My higher-self connects to the angel or guide. If I'm channeling a message, I also link to the Universal Field and the Akashic records to read past lives.

In prayer, you are creating a link to God. The crown on the top of your head opens to allow for divine light to instruct you. I always pray before I channel a message so I can become a vessel of light. With intention, I surround myself with divine light, I imagine roots reaching into the earth and I ask permission by saying, "Allow me to connect with my angel and the client's angel with the highest good of all." Notice it's for the person's highest good, which means it's not for my agenda.

Have you ever been given great advice you didn't take? Angels guide us into a course of action, but we don't always listen to it. Many clients tell me they were getting signs for weeks before I channeled for them, but didn't listen until they heard the same message from me. I love the look of surprise on a client's face dumbstruck by the *coincidences*.

Since I see clients for Reiki sessions, I'm open to light flowing in as I work. Since I'm an angelic channel, the angels will guide me while I do Reiki and will nudge me if there is something I'm supposed to say to the client. While working with Reiki, my heart chakra is wide open and in a state of compassion. Reiki is a powerful experience for the client and for me, bringing healing to both of us.

When channeling angels, I follow a similar process, trusting the angels to screen any guides stepping in to communicate with me.

Dream of my Guide a Spirit Visitor

When we are asleep, our subconscious mind is open. Any thoughts we repress may spill out in the form of bad dreams or fears. We are also open to messages and visits from the other side. Like a dolphin, the doorway of my brain was wide open as I was in a state of hypnagogic sleep and can see visions. I've had this weird sleep condition since childhood. It's worse if I'm stressed.

One evening, I fell into a deep sleep. I woke, my eyes opened, and before me stood a giant sized seven-foot tall guide wearing a white mask. His energy was kind and I had no fear of him.

This masked guide informed me that I was on a spiritual path and I was a '13' and my son is too. I researched number 13 and I found this meant advanced or ready soul.

Hypnagogic sleep is the experience of the transitional state from wakefulness to sleep: the **hypnagogic** state of consciousness,[3] during the onset of sleep. Mental phenomena that occur during this "threshold

---

[3] http://www.world-of-lucid-dreaming.com/exploring-your-hypnagogia.html

consciousness" phase include lucid thought, lucid dreaming, hallucinations, and sleep paralysis.[4]

Did you know that the Aboriginal people of Australia consider Dream Time more important than the time we are awake?[5] They believe that their dreams connect them to the world consciousness and the Field of Possibilities. They believe that they "dream the world into being." Without their dreams and meditation, the world would suffer. They are using group consciousness to raise world vibrations.

If you researched cave art, and you will find visions gained from astral travel. You'll see artistic symbols, and signs painted on cave walls in Australia and in many parts of the world.

Second sleep is the time between 5:00 and 6:00 in the morning, which is the most productive and prophetic time and one that yields greatest truth. Ayurveda medicine is a 3000-year-old healing system from India. The time between 5:00 and 6:00 in the morning is called the Psychic Doorway. [6]

We are more open while asleep, as our ego mind is not in charge.

In the Chinese culture, 3:00 am is the time when the liver clears. The liver holds anger. No wonder we wake at 3:00 am[7] especially when we're angry or troubled.

---

[4] https://en.wikipedia.org/wiki/Hypnagogia (Reference to lucid dreaming)
[5] http://www.aboriginalart.com.au/culture/dreamtime2.html
[6] http://en.ayurmed.org/lifestyle/dream-and-conciousness
[7] http://www.shen-nong.com/eng/lifestyles/tcmrole_health_maintenance_habits.html

Those that look outward dream, those that look inward awaken.

- Carl Jung

Nightmares— the Dark horse runs wild

The nightmare, gallops in and makes us tremor, but it's only a dream. Remember this: light has more power than darkness, always. If you do get a spirit or scary image, remember that it has no power *over you than your own fear.*

In some of my most vivid dreams, I have had awful images of wizards with red eyes, witches, and other evil things. I have firmed up my state of mind so that if something appears, I yell it away with a prayer, "Be Gone. You have no power here. Only God has power."

Fear makes little things bigger. Scary things grow with fear. Think of a tiny worry that you continue to feed. Before long, it's twice the size.

In my thirties, I was frightened and facing a medical procedure. I fell into an exhausted and unsettling slumber and dreamed and saw a vision of the tall reaper.

When he left, in came a frightening grim reaper I'd had seen in old movies wearing a black cape and peering at me with glowing red eyes. Call it a hallucination or a visit. In either case… terrifying. I think this scary vision was a gatekeeper to test my bravery and metal. I'd like to say I was brave, but I wasn't.

My faith flew out the window when in my paralyzed cataplexy sleep state and my body couldn't move. He touched my forehead with his long-fingered hand and mocked me with a chilling voice. "You'll die if you have an operation." Then it laughed at me. I was so scared that I broke out in a cold sweat, desperately trying to wake myself. I couldn't.

This was the worst vision and night terrors I've ever experienced. What's happening to me? I wondered. Was this a powerful lesson about fear and faith? I'm sure it was. Once the vision disappeared, I was unable to shake the scary image from my mind. For days I had trouble sleeping for fear of a second visit. I was afraid to channel.

After much prayer and contemplation, I realized that the reaper was a soul test. Why else would the masked guide show up first to tell me all those kind things if not to encourage me to fight the upcoming fear fest?

Since I had just started channeling angels, I realized the reaper was sent to test my fear. If it could scare me from my path for good, I'd not continue channeling. I failed miserably that night, but not for very long.

I decided to continue to advance and fight my fear with faith. This dark night of the soul wouldn't win. Fear wasn't an option for me any longer. I prayed for protection and decided to continue to channel angels. With my medical procedure looming ahead of me, I had faith that God would protect me.

Two weeks later, the specter appeared again, but was half its prior size! This time, ready for it, I demanded, "Be gone. God rules here!" It left. It returned one more time. On its last visit, it had decreased to a one-foot tall cloaked person still taunting me. It said, "If I can't have you, I'll get him instead." Then it pointed toward my sleeping husband and stood by his head.

The next morning my husband said he had awful nightmares of pure evil and dread. I knew what had caused it.

Did the vision have true power? No. *My fear gave it power over me.* Once I chose prayer, the fear, and the scary vision decreased and lost its hold. I re-claimed my power and my path.

The angels always instruct me to "Fear not and trust God." I advised my husband pray before he fell asleep. He complied and had a solid night's rest. The scary visitor never returned.

I Met a Guide in Person

I worked with guides and had an unusual dream. First, I've dreamed of my Indian spirit guide and a white wolf. The next day I was at a convenience store in New Jersey.

A long-haired Native American man stopped and stared at me as if peering into my soul. He wore a wolf shirt with a white wolf on it. You could have knocked me over with a feather.

It's highly uncommon to see people of Native descent. Was this a coincidence? A sensation of tingles ran down my spine. I heard his thoughts although no words passed between us. What did I hear? "Keep up the good work."

I believe we are lucky enough to see our guides we when we least expect to. As I progressed, I continued to search for a secret which eluded me.

I've learned to pray and ask for direction and guidance. Many of us pray. Listen to your intuitive guidance. Praying isn't just asking and telling God what we want.

Rosemary DeTrolio

Chapter 6
Angel Experiences

Back in 2000, I started Hands of Light by Rosemary LLC. I prayed to ask for healing information and guidance for my path and my business. With a rare free day ahead of me, I drove into Pennsylvania after feeling a strong urge to go there.

With my intuition to guide me, I thought, why not? As soon as I paid the toll for PA, I got a sudden push to drive toward the flea market.

Along my drive to the flea market, I received bits of information appearing in my mind. This inner nudge urged me to stop by the rocks and crystals table to buy a pendulum.

Since I had no desire to do this before that morning, I decided there must be a reason for this message. Curious, I followed my guidance. The thought popped into my mind. I'd meet a rock healer who would tell me something important. Even before I arrived, I had faith he'd be waiting there for me. I had a myriad of questions in my mind as I drove up to park. I'd wondered how to pick out the right pendulum, how I'd use one, how to clean a crystal, and how my business would fare.

My mind raced ahead with questions I'd ask him. As I walked to the crystal and rock table an old man with a black fedora and very intense blue eyes waved to me, then walked over to me.

He smiled with kind eyes and said, "I know about rocks and crystals and I've been waiting for you to arrive."

He looked into my eyes and told me how my heart was faring. I'd been getting twinges in it, but I never told him. I stared at him awestruck as he handed me a crystal pendulum and said, "This one will work well with your energies well. It will not lie to you."

I was incredulous and asked, "How did you know I needed this?"

He answered, "I am a metaphysical rock healer." You could have knocked me over with a feather. He answered all the questions I thought while driving, but didn't ask him. He looked into my eyes and said, "Do not ever bury a crystal to clear it, use water so it will not take on lost spirits from the earth." He then said, "Your heart is saddened. You need to worry less and trust God more. Your heart is fine." He hugged. "God blesses you for your work."

I thought, "He must be an angel." I handed him a business card hoping for a direct line to heaven. He walked away, and my eyes followed him. He literally disappeared into the crowd. I am convinced that he was an angel. Curious, I asked my angels about my strange encounter. They said we entertain angels unawares. I know it's true. We have guidance available to us in times of deepest need or strongest intent. The angels verified my meeting with the following reply.

May 8, 2001

I need to know if I spoke to an old man or angel. Who was he?

Is the sky a parcel of heaven; does the gate of the Lord open only one way? It is the seeker that finds, the child of God that sees possibilities. Be the wondering heart that searches out truth in open passages. Onstot the Wise One, angelic in nature. All can find truth veiled in mystery.

Tests come in wearing many faces; tests of trust, learning, openness all present themselves to those who are on the path. Guidance wears many faces, both human and seemingly human, as the one who walks the path is not alone.

It would be far easier for us to wear wings and show our glory, yet what would human kind really learn? The test of faith walks on silent shoes, it is not necessary to prove, as faith is the quality of one who believes.

The wish to know pure intent sends a clear signal out to the force of angels. God hears all prayers. God hears all intent, spoken and not spoken. Once intent is manifested, it rides the winds to God and is heard. Did you not ask for assistance? Did you not expect an answer? What is so difficult to understand?

I am excited and in awe of meeting the man in such a timely way.

And one, which you called for, through intent and prayer, was sent to you. You now see how much power thoughts hold. Intent is powerful; it is a creative manifestation of thought.

Be careful of thought and intent. May they be wise and loving… as all intent sends a message out to the universe and we hear it.

May I speak to that angel now?

The seven energy centers vibrate at speeds of color and healing. One must focus upon the centers with intent to check inner balance. The color of the rays, the stones can balance with each center. As intent is clear, so may be the messages. **(end)**

Like the man who showed up at the rock stand years ago, angels and guides can manifest, but only for short times and for certain reasons. I believe his appearance verified my dream and he was an angel.

In my angel communications, I've learned when a soul opens on earth, a rose will bloom in God's garden. The rose fragrance reminds us of God's garden, our true home. Roses have a vibration of 320 Hz. I grow roses to honor God for giving us angels, spiritual guides, avatars, and kind friends. Roses also resonate with the highest frequency of energy of any flower on earth, 320 MHz. The human brain resonates at 40 Hz in Beta. The human body resonates at between 62 and 72 Hz.

I feel close to God when I garden. How can anyone doubt the existence of God who has planted a seed? A tiny seed, which bursts into a plant, is a miracle to me. Even at age six, watching a lima bean seed emerge from a cup, I knew I had witnessed a miracle in the making.

When I was twelve year-old, my dad's friend Joe, found a constant companion in me, the pint-sized twelve-year-old future organic gardener wannabe.

Even at a young age I had a strong conviction to protect the earth. Chemicals were not an option in my garden or on my lawn. Joe taught me how to use natural fertilizer, soap water, grass clippings, and mulch. I learned how to make manure 'tea' to fertilize my plants. He instructed me how vegetables were companions with each other; such as basil and tomatoes, onions and peas. He grafted several types of apples on one tree explaining how to graft. Imagine three types of apples on one tree! I saw it.

I decided to start my own garden. Mom and I headed to the garden center for soil and manure. When we arrived home with 50 pounds of manure, my dad just about fell over laughing. "What are you going to grow with 50 pounds of shit?" He said through tears running down his face. To this day, I can't garden without remembering Joe's advice or dad's hysterics upon seeing 50 pounds of poo for a ten foot garden plot.

Coincidently, my other dear friend, also named Joe, helped me with garden questions when I moved my home after divorce. We exchanged gardening advice as well as recipes for making things like Cardoons, an Italian favorite known as Burdock. The large furry leaves have edible stems, which you string, cut, and fry in olive oil after breading them with parmesan and breadcrumbs. I remember how thrilled dad was to see this wild edible growing on the outskirts of my property.

The earth brings us together, and to the earth, we return.

In the years since, my garden blooms with vegetables, flowers, herbs, butterflies, dragonflies, and birds. Sometimes I plop right down in the dirt and sit there, sucking up nature. Winged creatures remind me of the spiritual nature of the soul. When I'm frustrated, pulling weeds is the best therapy for angst.

Tending to the garden is a grounded experience.

God uses people to convey messages to us. While at an Indian pow-wow, the vendor called me over and handed me a Native American angel tree topper. "This is for you," he said, "Spirit wants you to have her." That deerskin angel sits on my tree each year as a reminder of spirit's unexpected gift. At another event, a native man called me over to gift me with a bear claw. As we walked around, my friend commented that every single native person, man and woman stopped to stare at me as if seeing something around me. I was too busy looking at the beautiful objects for sale. When she mentioned it to me, I joked and said, "They probably see my aura."

Notice the difference between the guide's style, the angels, and mine. I channeled this message after the chance meeting with the Native wearing the wolf shirt.

Guide Message

The way of the wind, the Tao, the right path all lead to one place; different footsteps, different journey; the same destination. You see, the journey does not make the destination right or wrong. Religion is the journey.

The spiritual nature of humanity chooses many paths. If the destination to God is the same, then all are equal; if the path does not lead to God, then it is in error of truth. Many choices leave the path open so that all may find home with God.

It is not the particulars of the journey that make it correct or not. The journey is made by a loving gesture of good intention, doing no harm to any living thing, loving each other, and honoring the self in healthy ways.

The ego driven human will seek to self-gratify, prove others wrong, win a battle of wills, all useless activity, all detracting from the truth. Those who fight to be right are in error of truth. Those who seek to control are in error of truth.

God is the truth. The existence of the light beings is only debated by the humans on the earth plane!

How can a soul argue that something does not exist that is the very fact of its creation; a paradox, a trick, an illusion that simply distracts the unready ones, a parody, a foible of the existence. Does an egg debate whether its mother laid it? Does an oak tree doubt its start as an acorn?

Yet the debates have continued. Just when a debate is resolved, then humans argue over which religion is right, which path is the one. Do you see the foible?

Therefore, waste no time convincing, waste no effort that would detract one from God. Do not fret if those unready do not understand, as truth is not in error and not all will understand truth. Loving child, I am happy you called out to me today. Darius **(end)**

Chapter 7
Animal Totems and Spirit Animals

Thishis is a message that I received from my guide in 2004…

Can you speak about animals' souls?

Pure instinct, not ego driven; they are the essence of the wild nature. They have souls and can complete cycles of life, yet they are not made human, as some cultures believed. They have qualities inherent in the human soul, personified as separate entities, for example, the strength of the tiger, the wisdom of the hawk, and the playfulness of the chimp. They remind human kind of the soul qualities which make up humanity.

Did some Native Americans enter in animals through meditation?

Soul travel, yes. The astral soul may temporarily leave the body carriage as it does in sleep, at times. The astral soul may enter the animal realm to experience the essence of the animal soul, as many shamans have done. They understood the connection between all living things. We give homage to our winged ones, four foot, and all our ancestors. **(end)**

Soon after, I adopted a dog, which turned out to be part Dingo Wolf. Wolves fiercely protect, love, and guide their pack. When coincidences pile up, it's the angels sending you a message.

That Christmas, we received a wolf picture as a gift. A short time after, I was given three different wolf statues from unrelated people who had no idea I liked wolves.

My husband and I both are strongly attracted to wolves. We have a strong bond with each other, just like wolves do with their mates. Many Native tribes have a totem or clan animal to represent their tribe, such as a wolf, bear, turtle, and so on.

Hawks are amazing birds and one of my favorites. When I was a child, my spirit flew in the body of a hawk during a very lucid dream. At 17, my first airplane ride over the mountains was a familiar bird's eye view! Hawks have circled my home, have swooped down over my car countless times. I found hawk feathers in my yard.

My angels have told me that the hawk spirit reminds me to see the big picture, the overall view. Hawks have keen senses and are known as spiritual birds.

Animals protect our spirit and guide us with important life direction. It's uncanny how these wolves and hawks have made their way into my life.

Think about an animal you like. Maybe you collect statues or pictures of it or dream about them. Research the meaning for your totem animal to determine if there's a connection to your life. Many books and internet sites are available so that you can research the meaning of an animal messages. For example, a red fox that looked right at me, then turned tail and trotted away. I researched the fox totem. The fox is a messenger to remind me to be shrewd in dealing with people. Since I'm a trusting person, the fox gave me a lesson. Now my clients sign a disclaimer before I do a reading for them.

When my garden filled with a small family of snakes, I found the snake represents transformation. I examined my life. Snakes did appear at a crossroads.

Back in the 90's I had just moved into my home, as single parent with an eight-year-old son. Thirteen red-tailed hawks circled my home. Soon after, my dove dreams began. Next, a family of mourning doves moved into the trees around my home.

At one time, ten families of mourning doves were present. Doves are a sign of God's love and a symbol of Jesus. My land was being blessed. Within the next year, I met my husband.

Try Native Sacred Path cards or Totem animal divining cards for animal messages. Think of a question. Pull a card from the deck to see which animal presents itself.

Last, be kind to animals. I feed the birds and organic garden to give homage to nature. The animals appreciate a safe place to visit and they repay me with messages and appearances.

Wolves, Hawks, and Doves

I've always had a strange connection with animals. I can be anywhere and the hawks and birds start coming around. When I lived in my first house, a small baby robin landed two feet in front of me and let me stroke the top of its head. I really felt that this was a sign that God was near me for support.

I love wolves and have dreamed of them. Soon after, during meditation I saw a Pathfinder car. My soul felt the message. I am a Pathfinder leading people to God just as wolves lead their pack.

In Native culture, wolves are pathfinders and teachers. Animals bring light and love to our souls.

God said, "Let there be light." And there was light.

Golden Light Meditation

Meditation opens our awareness. Try out this technique:

1. Sit down with a straight spine. Imagine giant tree roots growing from the bottom of each foot.
2. Send these roots to the center of the earth to ground you.
3. Next, imagine yourself residing in a clean bubble of golden light. Allow this light to wash over you and merge with the cells in your body.
4. Feel any negative emotions burn away and be replaced with the loving light around you. Breathe in slowly.
5. With intention ask, "I'd like to have guidance from my highest spiritual guide about any block or issue I need to clear. I ask my guardian angel to allow only my highest guide in."
6. Wait and breathe.

7. When you are done, give thanks and see the crown of your head close like a door.

Use these blank spaces to record your own experiences.

Chapter 8
Patterns

There are no accidents.

Coincidences are God's way of remaining Anonymous. You must notice the signs.

There are many ways spirit tells us we are in the flow. It could be repeating number patterns, feathers in your pathway, a book that falls off a shelf, a call out of the blue, or a chance meeting.

Numbers are patterns and signs so you notice them. The number pattern 11:11 is a wake-up call, a reminder from the Universe to begin on your path, find your purpose, and stop wasting time. The angels named my book as an opening invitation to your own path.

Right before I communicated with angels, the numbers 11:11 appeared on clocks everywhere. The numbers intensified so they showed up on store receipts. Either I'd spend exactly $11.11, or cashier 111 helped me with my order and it was on the receipt.

By the end of the week, the dashboard of my vehicle showed 11111111. I had to be blind not to notice these odd coincidences piling up. Finally, I admitted something strange was happening. "I get it. This is a sign." I said. That's when my curiosity about number patterns started.

I researched the meaning of 11:11. This sequence is a wakeup call to the soul's blueprint. It's like a cosmic alarm clock awakening a soul to its mission.

The 11:11 message is, "Hey you. Remember why you came here? Get started on your path." A memory deep inside me stirred. Did other numbers mean something, too? I was born at the hour of 11:56 5+6 is 11. Coincidence? I don't think so. Soon, my husband noticed 11:11 everywhere. Pay attention to any repetitious number sequence that you notice. It's a sign.

444 means that angels are near. You might wish to explore Numerology, The Tree of Life, Mystic Kabballah or a book called *Angel Numbers,* by Doreen Virtue Ph.D., and Lynette Brown, Hay House publishers. I enjoy using this handy reference.

The ancient Chinese system of I-Ching, based upon the chance, teaches that random events are predetermined, therefore not truly random. In chaos, comes order.

After I hurt my back on 9/9/99, I researched the meaning of nine. The number nine is a completion of a life cycle number and the start of a new chapter. Lately, the number 3 sequence repeats for me. I've discovered that three represents the sacred trinity.

You'll find patterns in Sacred Geometry, Crop Circles, Numerology, I-Ching, and in the Mystic Kabballah. Read about frequencies, healing musical tones, Fibonacci sequence, the Golden mean, and the interrelationship of color, sound, and light.

Labyrinth

A labyrinth is an ancient meditative pattern found throughout Europe and near churchyards. Some are circular; some resemble the shape of a brain cut down the middle. All are giant mazes heading to the center and then out again.

At a spiritual event, I walked a labyrinth feeling the pull to try this ancient practice. Walking one requires patience. Taking slow movements taught me to be patient, but I fought each step. I focused on slow breathe and walk, breathe and walk. As I padded along the path with hurried feet that needed to slow down, the lines of the labyrinth allowed me to find peaceful contemplation. But I can't say it was easy for me.

Mindfully, I counted my steps, fighting my urge to leap or take giant strides to finish faster. I decided to try it the right way. A slow meander is not a dash, so I slowed my steps. Did the turtle really win the race with the rabbit? I wondered.

Where did this urge to race come from? As I child, my steps were languishing. I was the little girl who'd stop to admire every flower along the sidewalk. I was the one late to school which distressed my mother and my teacher who waited on me daily. Why was I late? I'd collect special pebbles, stop to taste sweet honeysuckle flowers, skip, dance, and sing, but rush nowhere. I was last up that hill. The crossing guard waited for me every morning and say, "Finally…" when I arrived. The sweet slow journey, so long ago. How did I lose it?

"Why is Rosemary *always* late for school?" The teacher asked my mother.

Mom, who always shooed me out the door in ample time to reach school, penned my teacher a heartfelt note, which read, "Love can move mountains, but only God can get my child to move faster!" God has moved me faster, and now he wants to slow me down. She even paid my enterprising ten year old neighbor to drag me hand-in-hand to school. When did my slow approach into the world change to rocket speed? Do we all scurry like rats in the race?

Many people walked this labyrinth before me, evidenced by the offerings of coins, shiny shells, stones, and medals as a thank you. I knelt down to pray and offer a coin, the only one in my pocket.

The center spiral is an inner circle, which holds my gaze as my feet wind slowly around the curves. Where have I been, where am I headed, and how did I get there? It always leads me back to where I began. It is in this spiral we look inward. In the circle, remember that we are endless.

Circles and Squares

You may have noticed that circles live in the same universe as squares. A square has a sense of truth and order. It is logical, measured, equal, and perfect edged.

Squares have difficulty understanding the endless circle. I've noticed circles often fall in love with squares. The circle tries to soften the square's rough edges. Squares try to convince the circles to be more linear.

God has a sense of humor. Circles often marry squares. We've been together for so long, we're both octagons and our love is in good shape.

April 15, 2001 Angel Message
Is there a message for me today?

Live in the quest. The journey of the soul has brought you far. It is our contention that the journey does not stop here. Continue to explore and learn, as you are not done yet.

The journey needs to continue as you explore color healing, rocks, shamanism, world religions and connections with all humankind. Many paths converge, as your journey widens.

You will speak to many people, as your path is set in motion. Your desire to speak out has helped us to bring the name of God and angels to the forefront again. All who seek will find if good intention is to prevail.

All of God's children unite as a force of light to help others find their way. You are the pathfinder, the wolf mother, and the guide for others on earth. May they follow you toward light. Be at peace. Two Feathers. (**end)**

Even our dwellings can give clues. Explore Feng Shui and its connection between your home, your life, and your health. A water leak in the bathroom might refer to a money leak or bad spending habits. Perhaps your body is retaining water. In the study of Feng Shui, each room represents a portion of our life or health. For instance, the bedroom represents romance; the kitchen represents hearth, and so forth.

When my toilet backed up, it was more than coincidence that my body had been bloated and backed up too. Water and flood dreams continued until I figured out the message. When ants appeared in my kitchen, they reminded me not to let little things irritate me. Be aware of the signs that your own house is telling you and see if there's a pattern.

Listen to Dr. Mona Lisa Schultz on mind-body medicine called *Intuitive Healing.* I encourage you to read some of her materials and explore the mind body connection. Read the late Dr. Dyer's book called *The Power of Intention* to learn more. Think of how many people walk around with knee pain. Did you know that fear locks in the knees? If you have knee pain, examine fear you might be holding.

Synchronicities are coincidences with purpose. Did you ever notice how coincidences occur once your mind is set in a certain direction? For example, if you want to learn yoga, everywhere you look yoga posters appear. If you are interested in a healthy eating regime, articles and information about healthy foods will be everywhere.

The angels applaud efforts and lend a hand. Remember, the Bible states, 'Ask and Ye shall Find.' It's true. When you seek, you will find. The universal law is called the Law of Attraction, the shopping list for what you want in your life. But it also works in the negative if you spend time thinking of all the awful things you don't want to occur. This makes a magnetic signal too. Your intention becomes a radar beam of focused magnetized energies matching toward what you seek. Like attracts like.

Tune into your intuition. If you live anywhere long enough and your energy imprints in the space you live. Since we spend time in our homes, they imprint with our energetic fingerprint. Did you notice how buildings and home have a feeling to them?

If you buy a home from someone, their energy imprint lingers. I use sage to clear my home and workspace of stuck energies.

Thoughts are Things

Thoughts are things. They have the power to hurt or to heal, they can move nations, give hope and encouragement, or destroy. We create our own beasts with our anger, fear, and worry.

> *Sticks and stones can break my bones,*
> *but words can break my heart.*

I listened to a speech from a visitor representing the Guardian Angels of NYC[8] (the coincidence wasn't lost on me.) He spoke about the power words have, both negative and positive in people's lives. Words are

---

[8] Gaurdianangels.org NY City

powerful and create energy as we speak them. When we speak, our thoughts and intentions create and affect world energy and world karma. I've heard the same message many times.

Energy makes an imprint.

We have the ability to change the world with our thoughts! Just imagine harnessing the power of our free will. Words can help and heal, or injure and destroy. The bad news is words affect energy. All those negative and fearful messages are floating out there too.

How do you change around your thinking? First, turn the news off. It's mostly negative and fear evoking. Decide if you need this information overload cluttering your calm.

Next, make a list of your positive qualities. What do you say to yourself? Are they positive, such as "I am a kind person?" Do you downgrade yourself? Do you call yourself names if you make a mistake?

Take some time to put my book down and just let the thoughts filter in to your consciousness. If you could rewrite a script to replace a hurtful comment you said or heard, what would it be? When we re-frame the comment, we move past the emotion and into a powerful proactive state of manifesting.

Count your blessings and write what you are grateful for each day. Gratitude is powerful since it puts your soul in harmony and higher vibration. The more you notice, the more you will see. Soon, the higher vibration you create changes your physiology.

Your body won't lie to you and bypasses the thinking mind. When you insist someone is a pain in your neck, don't be surprised if your neck aches. Can't stomach your job? You might set yourself up for colitis. Be careful how you speak your truth. Do so with kindness and integrity.

Our words, emotions and experiences lodge within our bodies. Our body does not lie to us about repressed emotions. Our body won't let us forget that something is bothering us. Our bodies scream at us to notice what we refuse to acknowledge. Stuffing down emotions wreaks havoc on our bodies. Notice your words, what you do and say. Think of how you phrase your words. What messages are you broadcasting to your body? What vibes do you send to other people?

Words have the power to both destroy and heal. When words are both true and kind, they can change the world.

- Buddha

Chapter 9
The World is a Mirror

Be sure you like what you see. Notice your emotions, judgements, and dislikes. If you distrust everyone, examine your perceptions and beliefs about other people. Are you contributing to this view by not being a trustworthy person in all of your dealings? Do you send fear and worry energy? Do you focus on thoughts that someone will cheat or deceive you?

> *Like thinking attracts like experiences.*
> *Universe will send you situations to prove you are right.*
> *Thoughts carry a vibration.*
> *Like a magnet, the situation and the person attract.*

It's true you can beam love like a beacon and still have negative people or unpleasant situations. Make a choice to stay in your own positive and hopeful mindset rather than allow the other person's fear to change your mood. The choice lies in how you react to negativity and what you chose to do about it.

Negative people develop a bad habit of shielding themselves even when the situation doesn't warrant it. Maybe they were disappointed by life, harbor poisonous resentments, regrets, or were physically or emotionally harmed. They have inner healing and self-love to practice.

Their wounds might be deep. Perhaps they can't forgive the person who helped create this emotional wound. We're all here to learn something. Don't take the other person's mood personally or judge. Don't allow the emotional dump to land on you. Bad moods are 'catchy,' but so is love and compassion. Compassion helps us to understand and forgive each other.

The universe mirrors our own intentions. If you don't like the life in front of you, change who's looking back at you. With gratitude and positive thinking in your life, you'll love the reflection you see within yourself and within your life.

Did you ever notice that when you are in a happy frame of mind, positive events seem more plentiful? Likewise, did you also notice that when you face your day on the "wrong foot" negative events continue to replicate? This is a Universal Law. Where thought goes, energy follows. This Universal Law is why porcupines are always prickly. They manifest situations to prove they are right and the Universe matches their vibration. The Law of Attraction is a Universal Law, which means it always works. How you use it is up to you.

You've heard the saying, 'birds of a feather flock together'. It's true. Be an eagle, not a turkey. Like attracts like. Your energy and vibration will match other similar energies in the Universe. Similar energy returns to you like a boomerang. The Universe mirrors our intentions. We place cosmic orders all the time, without realizing it.

For example, when we say, "I want money" we send out the "*want* of money." What you desire is abundance. If you think, feel, and act as if you are already abundant, you'll draw it to yourself through the Law of Attraction.

Instead of thinking you need money, focus upon abundance. Say, "I am already abundant and the Universe/God sends me financial abundance and blessings easily and quickly for my highest good." It's the feeling and belief that makes the magic happen.

All thoughts have energy and the world is a magnet and a mirror. Since time only exists in our mind, the Universe only understands "now". If you send your prayer as if it's already on its way, you will have unlocked the key. Your brain is hard wired not to know the difference between a real and fake. Our thoughts and imagination become a virtual reality machine. When you dream, it's not real, but it seems real.

Did you know your heart rate goes up when you watch a thrilling movie? Think of biting into a lemon. Your salivary glands react to your imagination. Listen to your thoughts. Notice how you might have been driving your own experiences.

Ponder how you react when your feelings are hurt. Do you lash out? Do you bristle with anger? Do you nurse a grudge or defend your point of view constantly? All takes effort and energy to hold a grudge.

If you have a prickly family member or co-worker, you can't avoid them. Join the club! We all have a person who can wear the description 'porcupine' on their lapel. Instead of getting caught in the web of angst, best to adjust your own perception and do your best not to engage in their drama.

Negative energy is prickly. When I'm near a porcupine, I sense daggers or points in his or her energy field. Porcupines don't mean to be prickly, but it's a learned behavior crying out for you to notice them. "Can you see me? Can you feel my pain?"

Their actions do just the opposite when they complain, yell, and throw fits so we avoid them. Who wants to hug a porcupine? It's a challenge if you love a porcupine or have one as a mate or a child.

Negative people lost sight of hope. They live in a cycle of self-imposed negative thought patterns. Porcupines think they control hurt by pushing others away. But they want connection, not isolation. They push away the very thing they desire— your love, compassion, and understanding.

If you find yourself with a porcupine, protect yourself from their drama. Don't match their negative energy with your own. Have compassion for them, but watch for those quills. Love energy is the only thing capable to lift a porcupine. If you can't love them at least pray for them. Limit contact and try again.

Positive communicators discuss issues but don't attack personalities. There is a difference. Only insecure people attack a personality. If you find yourself quilled by a porcupine, back up and don't react until you are centered and calm. Remind yourself that porcupines are clueless communicators.

They are probably hurting and might need a hug. When I hear a careless comment, I've used this technique. I repeat the person's comment very calmly so that they can hear it back. Then I walk away and let the comment sit. Often, the clueless porcupine is left alone with to mull over their careless comments. Sometimes I get an apology.

Choose to send love in the face of negativity and see what happens. When all else fails, spend less time with the negative person. You'll be amazed at the shift a relationship can take. Each positive choice you make for yourself creates a ripple effect upon humanity, like a stone in a pond.

Turning the other cheek works for a while, but soon you'll be spinning in a circle. Take positive actions instead, such as prayer, walking in nature, or calling a positive friend. A self-centered person caught in their own web doesn't realize how words can snare you. It's ok to take a break.

Communicate how you feel, then step back, take a deep breath, and let it go. The more you ruminate their words, the stronger the negativity gets. Untangle and do something else.

Struggle develops character.
A butterfly helped out of its chrysalis will die.
Coal turns to diamonds under pressure.

Chapter 10
Good Vibe Magnet

Shift your own mood by doing small acts of kindness for other people without expecting a return. This act of goodwill is for God, not for the person in that awful mood. For a day, pretend you are an optimist. Put on their rose-colored glasses and act as if you were that person. How does it feel to release all negativity? How does it feel to see the world as a safe place?

Do the good deed, but keep it anonymous. The deed is for the universe, not for your own glory or benefit. If I tell you what I did, it wouldn't be anonymous. I have some ideas you might try.

When you are at your favorite coffee shop, buy a coffee for the person behind you. If you see and old man or woman alone in a restaurant, buy dessert or pick up the check. Help someone load his or her groceries. Say hello, smile and thank people for the good job they are doing.

Good deeds are like seeds in a garden. They lay in wait and when you least expect it, you'll be surprised by a beautiful bloom.

Just like that flower, good deeds return in unusual ways. Blessed by kind unexpected gestures, and thankful for each one, we contribute to the greater good when we join in. It helps the giver and receiver feel great. It raises the vibration for both. What you sow you also reap.

When each person makes an effort to help each other, the 'world view' is uplifted and perception shifts. You remind people the world can be a good place and that the world is full of kind and caring people. Random acts of kindness are small inspired gestures.

Plant seeds of kindness to make your blessings bloom. Don't have any expectations of a return or outcome for your good deed. Expectation cancels the positive intent. Resentment kills the seeds. Just do it for the sake of joy. No expectation, no resentment. I'm a kid and animal magnet. If I'm in any public place, a child approaches to hang on me. A lost dog visits, a cat jumps up on my lap, or a child approaches me. Children and animals can sense good vibes. Since I was very young, people share their personal life stories with me. I intend to send good vibes whenever I go.

My father and I had this magnetic juju in common. Little did I know at the time; these early formative situations were clues to my adult life path to help people. The love energy has an irresistible vibration.

To my big-hearted friends, be aware we are also magnets for a narcissist or other selfish folks who find our caring energy irresistible. When you learn to have strong self-esteem and healthy boundaries, you'll notice them coming your way. If not, it's a long road with many tears.

My sister and I referred to our dad as a big loveable Saint Bernard dog — loud, friendly, open-hearted, and non-judgmental. My dad brought sunshine, laughter, and cheer with him everywhere he went. He loved to tell jokes and would often forget the punch line, which was funnier than the joke itself. Laughter followed dad like a happy puppy dog and people were drawn to him.

A constant barrage of people used to exhaust me, but not my dad. He loved the crowds and lived for them. He entered heaven like a child in

2007. His presence was so strong, I still feel him around and I laugh at his jokes and dad quotes.

Chapter 11
Lucid Dreaming

Lucid dreaming is aware dreaming. Part of the brain is awake, yet the door of consciousness is wide open. I've experienced lucid dreams as far back as I can remember.

The most vivid dream happened when I was eight-years-old. I visited the Hall of Records and could read past life scrolls. I heard a booming voice say that I'd have full access to them as an adult, but I wasn't ready for them yet. I still remember the commanding voice. That dream stuck with me all these years and I know those scrolls were blueprints and life charts I read when I channel for someone.

Sometimes unexplained fears are due to tragic experiences from a past life. In another repeating lucid dream is the giant wave ready to drown me. I believe I had a past life in Atlantis when it went under water. In my dream, I'm swimming away from a disaster trying to stay afloat.

At a young age, I'd panic if my face got wet in a swimming pool. Washing my hair was a disaster for my mom. I was terrified of the ocean waves and would scream if my face got wet. My mom wouldn't stand for it. At six, she took me for swimming lessons and my fear disappeared.

My friend is a hypnotherapist. I asked her to regress me twice to allow old memories to surface and clear them from my soul.

Did you know that it's possible to train yourself to have lucid dreams? My first experience of intentional lucid dreaming occurred when I was twelve. I had a re-occurring dream of being chased, but I never saw who or what chased me. I'd wake up breathing heavy and in a cold sweat. Bothered by this constant dream and I decided to research how to stop them.

I visited the local library and scan the shelves (before the invention of the Internet). I came across the perfect book. One passage gave me a solution to my nightmare troubles.

I learned and practiced a technique so I'd know when I was dreaming. I soon realized I held the power to change the outcome of my dream while it's in process. During a nightmare, a lucid dreamer can recreate an experience, leave the dream, or change its outcome. This was just the right information I needed to get rid of the scary chasing dream that had been plaguing me. Upon further reading, if an animal pursues, it may be a totem animal (spirit guide) trying to give a message. Armed with this new solution, I vowed to practice and learn the technique from the book.

Each day for two weeks, I repeated, "I will remember my dreams." The theory is that the message filters down into the subconscious layers of the mind through repetition and the visual cue of staring at your hands while awake jogs the dreamer into a lucid state.

That book stated that Native American parents taught their children to master dream fears as soul tests. Finally, I found an answer to my chasing dreams. The next time a chase dream started, I forced myself to stop running away, turn around, and face or fight whatever it was. I faced my fear and it had no power. Once I turned around, nothing was behind me! I was afraid of my own personal power.

Soon after, the chasing dream returned. I willed myself to stop running even though all of my instincts told me to dash away. I saw my hands in my dream so I was lucid. I forced myself to stand still, turn around, to face my nemesis. To my surprise, *nothing was behind me.* In that moment, I discovered that my greatest fear was harnessing the full power of my soul. At twelve, the truth flashed into my mind like a bolt. The mysterious entity chasing me was my *future mission and future self.* The intuitive recesses of my soul understood the message. The chasing dreams stopped.

I learned that we co-create our earth experiences and we can do this during dreams and after death. Our body does not tether our souls after death. Rules of gravity and physics no longer apply, just like in our dream state. We can't lose our body during a dream as we are always attached to it by a silver chord which I saw in a dream even before I knew what it was.

It wasn't until my 30s I fully grasped the importance of my realization of what my personal power meant. As an adult, my path has always been teaching, intuition, communicating with angels, and reading the Akashic Records life scrolls for other people. God revealed my path when I was eight years old and I never forgot visiting the Hall of Records.

During my best lucid dreams, I can fly.

According to the article cited below, there are four distinct realms of spirit, which are Physical, Quantum, Astral, and Ethereal. We live in the physical realm, but upon death, we spend time in the quantum realm, a place between heaven and earth. The astral realm is where thought forms and intentions are, and the ethereal realm is the place where higher consciousness lives.

I enjoy learning about ancient cultures and the wealth of spiritual wisdom they hold.[9]

Dream Recall

Dreams occur every night, even when you can't remember them once you wake. Try setting an alarm for 4:00 am, then fall back to sleep. Write what you remember in your journal. Try sniffing lavender on a cotton ball before bed, and then sniff it once more in the morning. Sometimes its scent will awaken your dream memory.

Vitamin B6 helps me see vivid dreams, but valerian root gives me unsettling creepy dreams. I've read that Mug wort tea to help with dream recall, but you'll have to see what works for you.

Before bed, meditate or pray to calm yourself. I like Linden tea to relax me. In cold weather, a hot Epsom salts bath makes me sleepy. It has magnesium in it, which calms my muscles down. Say a protection prayer, relax your mind and enjoy peaceful dreams. Try wordless music at bedtime. Keep a pen and pad by the bed to write impressions and feelings upon awakening. A dream cycle is typically 90 minutes long. Some people

----

[9]http://www.worlditc.org/f_02_macy_spirit_world_realms_0.htm

journal as soon as they wake up. The longest dream cycle is the last one before the morning and is usually the one you will remember the most.

Each morning, when the alarm goes off, close your eyes. Feel the emotion of the dream. You may recall small bits and images that stand out to you. The Buddhists refer to dreams as Wisdom Dreams and Karmic Dreams.[10] Karmic dreams clue you in to your life lessons and your shadow self. We label them as "bad" when they are shedding light on fears and lessons. Wisdom dreams are usually lucid ones.

Dream symbols are unique to each of us. Dream books aren't helpful. Keep a dream journal to decipher your own symbols. The most telling parts of a dream are your emotions, your symbols, and images, not necessarily the crazy content. The tone of your dream is the greatest clue about its meaning for you.

Some basic symbols are archetypes. Common dreams happen for all of us. Have you had a dream where you were falling? Did you die in your dream, or lose teeth? Remember, dreams are symbols for our emotional state. See how the images apply to you personally. If they don't apply, compile your own list of your common dream symbols or images. The best time to list them is right when you awake.

Dreams show us our state of mind, or worries, and thoughts we've repressed during the day. It's healthy to dream. New learning is processed through sleep. The mind clears debris through dreaming. I call it 'clearing

---

[10] https://www.budsas.org/ebud/whatbudbeliev/321.htm

out the attic.' With my symbols, I've discovered anxious dreams tell me I've stuffed a worry down deep and need to examine my feelings.

The worst-case scenario dreams occur when I'm in a new situation. My dream brings me to the most ridiculous exaggeration of all that could go wrong. When I wake, I have a good laugh at my own expense.

As I stated in the last section, I have hypnogogic sleep. Under stress, the high emotions kick in the doorway and my attic opens wide.

Since our subconscious doorway opens during sleep, it's a perfect time for angels, guides, and loved ones to visit. For me, a visitation dream feels very real. The dream is clearer, in high-def color. The pace moves at earth time and isn't a jumble of random images.

Angels and guides communicate in our dreams. They don't have to speak but transfer messages through telepathy. Sometimes our loved ones will do the same.

Dreams, good and bad, cannot control us no matter how real they seem to be or how much they scare us. Our free will is present. Learn to lucid dream and you'll have even more control in your dream world.

When we are asleep, our subconscious mind is open and your whole brain of your mind is available, even the parts we can't access when awake.

When a dolphin sleeps, one-half of its brain controls swimming and functioning while the other part of the brain is in sleep mode. Dolphin's brains are huge. Ours brains are smaller, but efficient. Our subconscious acts like a vast computer remembering every face, thought, and experience. It's the key to our perception of our fears, our truths. But our soul holds the key to our true nature.

Shine a light where darkness lies. If you have a fearful dream, examine it. What is it trying to tell you? Ask yourself if there's an issue, person, or fear in your life you've repressed. Journal the emotion behind your dream and you will begin to unearth your own symbols and patterns.

Chapter 12
Remote Viewing and Astral Travel

I n theosophy and anthroposophy, the Akashic records are a compendium of all human events, thoughts, words, emotions, and intent ever to have occurred in the past, present, or future. They are believed by theosophists to be encoded in a non-physical plane of existence known as the etheric plane. *(Wikipedia)*

Astral travel is the ability to release your soul from your body and visit a chosen location. As an infant, I'd leave my body and fly on the ceiling seeing my diapered body crawling on the floor below. I was intrigued to learn more.

What have I seen in the astral plane?

I've visited the astral plane, a dismal gray and dimly lit realm, like twilight. I've seen wandering lost souls with vacant eyes, and frightening thought forms left over from the dreams of other people. In jest, I've wondered if author Steven King, is responsible for a bunch of them. The astral plane holds negative forms and stuck energies. I don't fear it, but I don't want to hang out there either.

If you find yourself wandering around, pray for the people who look like they are in a trance. These are ghosts; a shadow of a lost soul.

In some visits, I've tried to get the attention of a lost soul. I've pleaded, "You're dead. Look for the light! The angels will help you. Just ask." Sadly, they ignore me and continue to wander unaware of their condition accepting it as their lot.

As I mentioned, I experience hypnologic sleep. I often have thought that a schizophrenic episode must be like having the subconscious door wide open during waking hours. To research lucid dreaming: Stephen La Berge, Lucidity Institute on FB and the internet.[11] [12]

We can't lose our body during astral travel, any more than you can lose your soul in a dream. When you're lucid dreaming, you are able to program your subconscious. In the same way, when practicing astral travel, focus on a particular location while you meditate. I've met psychic mediums who use a form or link- up with a deceased soul meeting at a certain location.

Some experienced astral travelers can recall details of the location he or she visited during their experience. The details can be verified. Back in the 70s the government had a secret group of people working as psychic spies. I heard David Morehouse, a decorated army officer, speak about being a member of this elite program. This was the reason for training people to astral travel during the US spy program, according to David Morehouse. The astral travelers meditated to find certain locations in other countries, then drew the details.

---

[11] https://www.youtube.com/watch?v=IG-sDcQiqMI
[12] https://www.youtube.com/watch?v=rFjiAUYZj68

Read *The Psychic Warrior,* by David Morehouse.[13] He writes about a top-secret US project he was a part of in the 1970's. The members of this elite group practiced astral travel, remote viewing, and conscious dreaming for its application in spy warfare. The movie *Talking With Goats* spoofed this program.

At Omega Center in Rhinebeck, NY, I met Mr. Morehouse and listened to his fascinating experiences in this formally top-secret program. Check You-tube for his talks. You'll agree that truth is stranger than fiction. I found online classes he gives to learn remote viewing.

---

[13] http://davidmorehouse.com Remote Viewing site

Rosemary DeTrolio

Chapter 13
Love Yourself Like the Angels Do

Sometimes, people hear my stories and say, "What about me? Doesn't God hear my prayers?" I'm telling you that everyone has had these moments of doubt. The Universe will reward you with all kinds of signs, coincidences, and small reminders once you're aware of them. You'll also get proof only after you no longer require it, which is a paradox. Angels told me that belief comes before proof. The angels love you and remind us to honor our truth.

After my continued efforts to connect with angels, a Sanskrit or Latin word would appear in the communication. I'm sure they knew I'd attempt to define each word. I'd find out it was Sanskrit or Greek and would have an actual definition. One word I checked on meant, "dwelling house of the Lord."

I'm sure this was a little pat on the back as if to say, keep at it, kid. You're not making this up. Even with this small encouragement, I wrestled with myself. Looking back, I realize that my struggle wasn't to believe angels communicated with me, but to believe I was worthy to receive their words. We're all worthy to receive divine love, but I too had a bit of Doubting Thomas in my faith.

Angels infuse love into each communication. The love goes directly to the soul of the person who reads or hears them. It's like Cupid's arrow to the heart. I've witnessed big macho men break out in tears upon reading the angels words to them.

Thinking back, I know I was always guided. I was in middle school when I realized the vibes and energy around me. My friends said, "I knew stuff." They commented my extra sense was a little freaky. In jest, they'd ask if I was a witch. I didn't like this comparison and no I wasn't.

I had no desire to ghost bust or commune with deceased people. Even though it's not my path, Dad showed me his journey to the other side and his own experience when he crossed over. I believe my dad opened up a doorway for me. During Reiki, sometimes relatives show up for the client, very insistent. They pop by to blow smoke in my face, or insist I pass along a message to my client. My guess is that dad must have said to the spirits, "Go visit my daughter. She'll help you out!" These spirits aren't ghosts, they are loving relatives who are visiting.

I've dreamed of many relatives who have passed and have been able to give messages to my cousins and friends. Dad continues to help me from beyond.

In the Reiki healing system,[14] I use the Christ symbol and the protection light symbol on the client's crown chakra. I use Frankincense oil on the top of my head and my temples whenever I practice healing

---

[14] https://iarp.org/
International Asssociation of Reiki Practioners

work or meet for intuitive sessions. This essential oil repels any negative entities, but still keeps me open to receive angels.

I sage my home and office and have assisted on having a cleared space to work. If I'm at an event, I spray the area with lemon and Frankincense oil if I can't sage. I've felt stuck energy in public venues and have sealed a room before I'd work in it.

If your own mood is out of whack and you need help to clear yourself, see a qualified energy worker who specializes in ghost clearing, or see me for a Reiki session.

A few years ago, I attended a historic train station converted to a restaurant. I was in a foul mood since my husband and I had a disagreement. Remember my description earlier in this book about mood. My energy field was prickly. Before I knew it, exhaustion hit me. My energy field was a welcome sign for a soul of one ill-tempered old woman. I didn't feel like myself and my anger fueled. Most likely, the old woman had a bone to pick with men and my mood fed her disgust. Her presence made my mood worse. It took me a few hours to fully realize I had picked up a hitchhiker. I prayed and told it to leave me. And she did.

From this experience, I learned to stave off bad moods before they broadcast an invitation to bad tempered discarnate souls. Like attracts like.

Don't let this scare you. Sometimes we're just in a bad mood and it doesn't mean a ghost has attached to you. Keep your moods in check doing your best to be aware. Energy sends out a broadcast beam. Start each day with a positive mantra, intention, or prayer. Light is stronger than darkness.

You can research boogie busting or entity clearing. Get trained by a qualified person if you plan to ghost bust or communicate with ghosts. Don't talk with ghosts or play with Ouija boards, okay?

The only power a dark spirit has is our fear of it.
Fear is __F__alse __E__vidence __A__ppearing __R__eal

In closing, know that you are a special soul meant to be here. You have a purpose to fulfill and a life mission. Don't let fear stop you from your spiritual path. May you walk the path of joy all the days of your life and allow the angels of God to guide you.

Blessings and Light,

Rosemary

Do you have questions? Comments?

Visit my web site to learn more. Sign up for my mailing list at:

www.rosemaryd.com

Hands of Light by Rosemary LLC

God Bless You!

Definitions of Terms

Angels: The many souls, never human, assigned to do God's work. They have no free will, only God's will. They protect and guide us while we are on earth. They have never been human and were created when God created all souls. They are messengers and intermediaries between God and our soul.

Archangels: These are the 4 main angels mentioned in the Bible. They are Michael, Raphael, Uriel, and Gabriel.

Suruel, Raphael, Raguel, Michael, Gabriel, Remiel, and Uriel are mentioned in the Old Testament

Astral Travel: The soul can leave the body temporarily while attached with the silver cord. Some people travel while sleeping, some while meditating.

> *Monroe Institute Lucid dreaming information:*
> *https://tinyurl.com/y46te4hn*

Aura: The colors sent out by the seven charkas into the soul. This energy field is in us as well as around us.

Ascended Masters: Those deeply spiritual people who have passed on. They still guide and teach from the spirit world. Jesus is one example.

Chakras: Seven energy wheels that start at the base of the body and travel upward. There are more than seven chakras and new ones are opening. Minor chakras are on the palms and feet which open with the attunement to the Reiki healing system (which I teach and offer). Colors rotate and revolve, the energy feeds different organs and nerves of the body.

Channeling: This is a conscious connection of receiving information downloaded through the crown chakra to the soul from the Universal Consciousness.

Consciousness: The wisdom of the soul which continues to exist even after our death. While alive, this conscious energy permeates all of our vital organs and cells and effects the aura. Even the bacteria in your gut is a community of conscious cells.

Dreams: There are many types of dreams. While asleep, our subconscious mind is wide open and receptive.

Books about dreaming:

Sun Bear et al. *Dreaming the Wheel. How to Interpret your dreams using the medicine wheel.* Fireside 1ˢᵗ edition, 1980.

Cowan, James. *Mysteries of the Dream-Time: The Spiritual Life of Australian Aborigines.* Prism Press, 1993.

Forgiveness: Resentments create poison and toxins in our body. You release yourself from pain and distress when you practice forgiveness.

Free Will: God's law that angels must adhere and follow. They can guide, but we must choose and learn from our choices.

Gate of God: The crown chakra is the entry and exit for the soul. It is at the crown of the head.

Ghost: A stuck soul who has turned away from the light at the time of death.

Book about ghosts:

Bodine, Echo. *Relax, it's only a Ghost* Fairwinds Press, 2001

God: Known by many names, the creative force of light in all sentient and non-sentient beings, the Creator, the I AM presence.

Guardian Angel: This is the angel that has been created to protect your soul from sudden harm before your time on earth is up. Each soul has a Guardian angel regardless of belief, or religious background.

Higher self: This is your soul. Your soul houses all memories from this lifetime and previous ones.

Intuition: A natural ability we all have and use at different degrees. It is the link to the soul and can give us guidance through our dreams, flashes of insight, or ideas.

Inspirational Writing: Tapping into the white light energy to get guidance.

Law of Attraction: Our thoughts attract like energy and experiences. We manifest what we send.

Light: The light force of angels, spiritual guides, ascended Masters, and God energies.

Love: This is the highest goal for a human, love of self, love of others, true acceptance and non-judgement.

Manifesting: The process of drawing like energies and universal help to you by the use of positive thought, prayer, and focused intent.

Meditation: The awareness of inner self. Looking within during a calm and quiet state of mind.

Past Lives: Our soul is eternal and has had many experiences to learn while in different situations, different bodies, and often many of the same people we have met before.

Book about past lives:

Moody, Raymond. *Life After Life: The Investigation of a Phenomenon - Survival of Bodily Death*. Mass Market Paperback; 2001.

Protection: A practice of prayer, grounding, and clearing the energy field before doing spiritual work.

Protection Prayer: Prayer works to send light around the soul and the body. Prayer helps you to align with God.

Religion: A certain pathway or set of values and beliefs a culture holds and practices.

Shaman: Native American healer or one who contacts spirit.

Signs: That's God telling us we are on the right track.

Soul: The gift from God that resides in all of us. It is the way we connect ourselves to God.

Soul healing: Releasing lessons or pain held in the body from a previous, or same, existence.

Spiritual Guides: Spiritually advanced people who reached a certain state of awareness and enlightenment on earth and who have crossed over. They are assigned to guide us on our journey.

Toning: Sound used for healing.

Universal Knowledge: It comes from the God-source in the form of light beings, emissaries of peace and loving energy. The knowledge surrounds earth, enters through our crown, to our higher self and then into our minds.

References

Hands of Light by Rosemary LLC - http://www.rosemaryd.com
(This is my web site)

Baumann, Lee. *God at the Speed of Light*. Virginia: A.R.E. Press, 2002.

Bodine, Echo. *Relax, it's only a Ghost* Fairwinds Press, 2001

Brennan, Barbara. *Hands of Light. A guide to healing through the human energy field*. N.Y: Bantam Books, 1988.

Cowan, James. *Mysteries of the Dream-Time: The Spiritual Life of Australian Aborigines*. Prism Press, 1993.

Cocrane, A. and Cullen K., *Beyond the Blue, Dolphins and Their Healing Powers*. Bloomburg Publishing, 1998.

Dyer, Wayne. *The Power of Intention*. California, Hay House, 2005.

Emoto, Masaru, David A Thayne (translator) *Messages in Water*. Beyond Words Publishing, 2004.

Emoto, Masaru. Web site retrieved from
https://www.masaru-emoto.net/jp/

Farguherson (translator). *Meditations of Marcus Aurelelius Antoninus and a Selection of Letters of Marcus and Frotno* London: Oxford University Press 1998.

Hicks, Jerry and Esther. *Ask and it is Given*. California: Hay House, 2002.

International Association of Reiki Practitioners website. Retrieved from
http://www.IARP.org

Jung, Carl. *Dreams*. Princeton Press 1974

The Dalai Lama and Howard C. Cutler, M.C. *The Art of Happiness at Work*. New York; Riverhead Books, 2003

King, Jr., Martin Luther. *A Testament of Hope: The Essential Writings and Speeches of Martin Luther King Jr.* San Francisco: Harper Press 1990.

Matineau, John. *Mazes and Labyrinths in Great Britain*. England: Counter Culture Publishers, 1999.

Mc Gaa, Ed. *Rainbow Tribe; Ordinary People Journeying on the Red Road* San Francisco: Harper 1992.

McGraw, Dr. Phil. Personal website retrieved from http://www.drphil.com

McLearen, Karla. *Your Aura and Chakras; the owner's manual.* Weiser Books, 1998.

Monroe Institute Lucid Dreaming Information. Retrieved from https://tinyurl.com/y46te4hn

Moody, Raymond. *Life After Life: The Investigation of a Phenomenon--Survival of Bodily Death.* Mass Market Paperback; 2001;

Morehouse, David. *Psychic Warrior: The True Story of America's Foremost (Psychic Psychic Spy and the Cover-Up of the CIA's Top-Secret Stargate Program Warrior)* St. Martin's Paperbacks; Reprint edition. 1998

Native Totems website. Retrieved from https://tinyurl.com/jndy9mw

Omega website. Retrieved from http://www.Omega.org *(This is a wonderful organization with great classes)*

Orloff, Judith. *Intuitive Healing.* California: Hay House, 2002.

Rainbow Eagle website. Retrieved from http://www.rainboweagle.com/index.html

Schulz, Mona Lisa Dr. *Awakening Intuition: Using Your Mind-Body Network for* Insight *and Healing.* Three Rivers Press, 1999.

Take the Leap. Interesting organizations and sites: http://www.taketheleap.com/organizations.html

The Secret website. Retrieved from https://www.thesecret.tv/

Transformative Thought. Retrieved from https://trans4mind.com/

Saint Germaine, the Seventh Ray. Retrieved from http://www.crystalinks.com/stgermain.html

Sun Bear et al. *Dreaming the Wheel. How to Interpret your dreams using the medicine wheel.* Fireside 1st edition, 1980.

Talbot, Michael. *Holographic Universe* New York: Harper Perennial Press reprint 1992.

Thich Nhat Hanh. *The Heart of Buddha's Teaching* New York: Broadway, new edition 1999.

Virtue, Doreen. *Chakra Clearing.* California: Hay House; Book and CD edition, 2004

Virtue, Doreen. *Divine Guidance; How to have a dialog with your Guardian Angels.* Renaissance Books, 1999.

Virtue, Doreen. *Indigo Children.* California, Hay House, 2002.

Walker, Brian B., Jung, C.G. *I Ching book of Changes.* St. Martin's Griffin, reprinted. 1993.

ABOUT THE AUTHOR

Rosemary DeTrolio is a Reiki Master Teacher, angel communicator, and intuitive. She lives in a small town and is the owner of Hands of Light by Rosemary LLC where she teaches life enriching classes, holds private sessions, and guides people from all faiths to their path and purpose. She enjoys guest speaking, writing, and guiding people.

She spent 32 years in full time education mentoring new teachers She is a proud mom of an adult married son, and grandmother to an adorable little boy. She's married and lives with two dogs and a big fat cat and her husband.

www.rosemaryd.com

Made in the USA
Middletown, DE
15 October 2025

19169893R00076